TOOLS *(continued)*

Object-Manipulation Tools

⬚⬚⬚	Align
⬚	Group
⬚	Move to Back
⬚	Move to Front
⬚	Ungroup

View Icons

☰	Outliner
◢	Slide Editor
⦿	Slide Sorter

Miscellaneous Tools

▦	Data Form
Slide 8 of 8	Go to Slide
🚚	Symbol
⊙⁺	Zoom In
⊙⁻	Zoom Out

Other titles include *Up & Running* with:

AutoSketch 3

Clipper 5.01

Compuserve

CorelDRAW 2

dBASE III PLUS

DOS 3.3

DOS 5

DR DOS 5.0

Excel 3 for Windows

Flight Simulator

Grammatik IV 2.0

Harvard Graphics

Harvard Graphics 3

Lotus 1-2-3 for Windows

Lotus 1-2-3 Release 2.3

Lotus 1-2-3 Release 3.1

Mac Classic

Macintosh System 7

Norton Desktop for Windows

Norton Utilities

Norton Utilities 5

Norton Utilities 6

Norton Utilities on the Macintosh

PageMaker 4 on the PC

PageMaker on the Macintosh

PROCOMM PLUS

PROCOMM PLUS 2.0

Q & A 4

Quattro Pro 3

Quicken 4

ToolBook for Windows

Windows 3.0

Windows 286/386

Word for Windows

WordPerfect 5.1

WordPerfect 5.1 for Windows

XTreeGold 2

Computer users are not all alike.
Neither are SYBEX books.

We know our customers have a variety of needs. They've told us so. And because we've listened, we've developed several distinct types of books to meet the needs of each of our customers. What are you looking for in computer help?

If you're looking for the basics, try the **ABC's** series, or for a more visual approach, select **Teach Yourself.**

Mastering and **Understanding** titles offer you a step-by-step introduction, plus an in-depth examination of intermediate-level features, to use as you progress.

Our **Up & Running** series is designed for computer-literate consumers who want a no-nonsense overview of new programs. Just 20 basic lessons, and you're on your way.

SYBEX **Encyclopedias** and **Desktop References** provide a comprehensive reference and explanation of all of the commands, features and functions of the subject software.

Sometimes a subject requires a special treatment that our standard series don't provide. So you'll find we have titles like **Advanced Techniques, Handbooks, Tips & Tricks,** and others that are specifically tailored to satisfy a unique need.

You'll find SYBEX publishes a variety of books on every popular software package. Looking for computer help? Help Yourself to SYBEX.

For a complete catalog of our publications:

SYBEX Inc.
2021 Challenger Drive, Alameda, CA 94501
Tel: (510) 523-8233/(800) 227-2346 Telex: 336311
Fax: (510) 523-2373

Up & Running with Harvard Graphics® for Windows™

Rebecca Bridges Altman

SYBEX®

San Francisco • Paris • Düsseldorf • Soest

Acquisitions Editor: David Clark
Series Editor: Joanne Cuthbertson
Editor: Carol Henry
Project Editor: Barbara Dahl
Technical Editor: Charlie Russel
Word Processors: Ann Dunn, Susan Trybull
Book Designer: Elke Hermanowski
Icon Designer: Helen Bruno
Screen Graphics: Cuong Le
Desktop Production Artists: Claudia Smelser, Alissa Feinberg
Proofreader: Rhonda Holmes
Indexer: Ted Laux
Cover Designer: Archer Design
Screen reproductions produced with Collage Plus.

Collage Plus is a trademark of Inner Media Inc.

SYBEX is a registered trademark of SYBEX Inc.

TRADEMARKS: SYBEX has attempted throughout this book to distinguish proprietary trademarks from descriptive terms by following the capitalization style used by the manufacturer.

SYBEX is not affiliated with any manufacturer.

Every effort has been made to supply complete and accurate information. However, SYBEX assumes no responsibility for its use, nor for any infringement of the intellectual property rights of third parties which would result from such use.

Library of Congress Card Number: 91-68500
ISBN: 0-89588-1031-2

Manufactured in the United States of America
10 9 8 7 6 5 4 3 2 1

SYBEX
Up & Running Books

The Up & Running series of books from SYBEX has been developed for committed, eager PC users who would like to become familiar with a wide variety of programs and operations as quickly as possible. We assume that you are comfortable with your PC and that you know the basic functions of word processing, spreadsheets, and database management. With this background, Up & Running books will show you in 20 steps what particular products can do and how to use them.

Who this book is for

Up & Running books are designed to save you time and money. First, you can avoid purchase mistakes by previewing products before you buy them—exploring their features, strengths, and limitations. Second, once you decide to purchase a product, you can learn its basics quickly by following the 20 steps—even if you are a beginner.

What this book provides

The first step usually covers software installation in relation to hardware requirements. You'll learn whether the program can operate with your available hardware as well as various methods for starting the program. The second step often introduces the program's user interface. The remaining 18 steps demonstrate the program's basic functions, using examples and short descriptions.

Contents and structure

A clock shows the amount of time you can expect to spend at your computer for each step. Naturally, you'll need much less time if you only read through the step rather than complete it at your computer.

Special symbols and notes

You can also focus on particular points by scanning the short notes in the margins and locating the sections you are most interested in.

In addition, three symbols highlight particular sections of text:

The Action symbol highlights important steps that you will carry out.

The Tip symbol indicates a practical hint or special technique.

The Warning symbol alerts you to a potential problem and suggestions for avoiding it.

We have structured the Up & Running books so that the busy user spends little time studying documentation and is not burdened with unnecessary text. An Up & Running book cannot, of course, replace a lengthier book that contains advanced applications. However, you will get the information you need to put the program to practical use and to learn its basic functions in the shortest possible time.

We welcome your comments

SYBEX is very interested in your reactions to the Up & Running series. Your opinions and suggestions will help all of our readers, including yourself. Please send your comments to: SYBEX Editorial Department, 2021 Challenger Drive, Alameda, CA 94501.

Preface

If you're in business—virtually any business—you're involved in presenting something to somebody, somehow, somewhere. And with a PC in your office, why not turn over the business of presentations to it? That's the foundation of desktop presentations in general, and Harvard Graphics for Windows in particular. Bullet charts, tables, org charts, bar graphs, pies—all grist for the presentation mill.

Harvard Graphics for Windows represents Software Publishing Corporation's first foray into the Windows 3.0 operating environment, and it's nothing short of a match made in heaven. Harvard no longer has to go about its business in a vacuum; instead, it can avail itself of all the tools that have made Windows 3.0 a success. Harvard can effortlessly borrow data from neighboring spreadsheets, or drawings from illustration packages. Any font outline you have installed in Windows shows up in Harvard's menus. All of the services provided by Windows and its applications are at your disposal as you sit behind the wheel of Harvard Graphics for Windows.

Every powerful program, including Harvard Graphics for Windows, requires training and practice; that's where this book enters the picture. *Up & Running with Harvard Graphics for Windows* covers all the major features of the program, with enough detail to get you up and running quickly. And, if you are coming over from the DOS version of Harvard Graphics, you will find this book to be a helpful and welcome transition.

Table of Contents

Installing Harvard Graphics for Windows on your computer is not difficult; Software Publishing Corporation (SPC) provides a guided installation that helps you through the process of copying the program files from floppy disks to your hard disk. Installation takes approximately 10 to 25 minutes.

One of the many advantages of using Windows is that you do not need to specify hardware devices (printers, video displays, and mice) when you install a new Windows application. Because you specify these devices when you install Windows, this configuration is set for use by all Windows applications, including Harvard Graphics for Windows.

Hardware and Software Requirements

To run Harvard Graphics for Windows on your computer, you need the following hardware and software setup:

- An IBM PC or compatible computer with an 80286, 80386, or 80486 processor

- At least 2 megabytes (Mb) of RAM; 4Mb is recommended

- From 7 to 13.5Mb of free hard disk space, depending on how much of the package you install

- One floppy disk drive (5 or 3½ inch)

- A graphics card with at least 256K of memory

- A Microsoft or compatible mouse

- A printer supported by Windows 3.0 (for example, PostScript or Hewlett-Packard LaserJet)

- Windows 3.0 or later

- DOS 3.1 or later

You will also need the disks that came in your Harvard Graphics box.

Running the Install Program

The Harvard Graphics for Windows disk labeled Disk 1 includes an installation program, called Install, that takes you through the process of copying the Harvard files to your hard disk. Follow these steps to run Install:

1. If necessary, load Windows. The Windows Program Manager should be active.

2. Insert Disk 1 into your disk drive.

3. Pull down the File menu and choose Run.

4. Type **A:\INSTALL** or **B:\INSTALL**, depending on which drive you are using.

5. Click on OK or press Enter.

You can also start the Install program from your DOS prompt.

Choosing Installation Options

Once the Install program is loaded, you will see the window shown in Figure 1.1. Here, you specify the path for the Harvard Graphics program files (C:\HGW is the default) and choose how much of the program you want to install: all files, the minimum file set, or selected files. Let's look at each of these installation options in detail; it's important that you understand the requirements and results of each one. Before you choose Install All Files, you should know what will happen in your system.

Installing All Files

Installing all files requires 13.5Mb of hard disk space and about 25 minutes of your time. (The time estimate in the installation window is an understatement.) The following items are copied to your hard disk:

*   Program files
*   All presentation styles

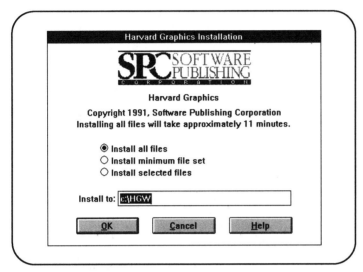

Figure 1.1: Harvard Graphics Installation window

- All color palettes
- The four Bitstream type families included with the program (Dutch, Geometric Slabserif, Swiss, and Monospace)
- All import and export filters
- All symbol (clip art) files
- Sample tutorial files
- The Autographix Slide Service utility

Don't worry if many of these items make no sense to you—you'll learn what they are as you read through this book.

Installing the Minimum File Set

Because installing all files requires so much disk space, you might want to consider installing the minimum file set, which requires only (*only?!!*) 7Mb. It consists of the following:

- Program files

- Two color palettes (default and monochrome)

- One default presentation style

- The four Bitstream type families included with the product (Dutch, Geometric Slabserif, Swiss, and Monospace)

- Several import and export filters (Harvard Graphics 2.x and 3.x, WMF, and BMP)

The minimum file set gives you a solid base for learning Harvard Graphics, and contains all the files many people will ever need. However, once you get to a more advanced level of use (as described in Steps 16 through 20), you'll probably want to add additional color palettes, presentation styles, filters, and symbols. At that point, you can run the Install program again and choose the Install Selected Files option. You can then choose which files to copy.

Finishing the Installation

Once you have decided whether you want to install all files or the minimum file set, click on the appropriate option, and then choose the OK button. Assuming you have sufficient disk space, the Install program copies the files from the floppy disks to the path you specified, prompting you when you need to switch disks.

Choosing a program group

When all the files are copied, a dialog box asks you where you want to place the icon for Harvard Graphics for Windows. The box lists the program groups on your system; just click on the group in which you want to store the icon. You can also enter a description for the icon, or accept the default name of Harvard Graphics. When you've entered the description and selected a group, choose OK. If you installed all files, you will see another, similar dialog box for designating the Autographix icon.

Finally, the Install program shows you the default paths for the Harvard Graphics files. This box gives you a good idea of where different files are stored, in case you want to remove some files you don't need. Notice that some of the files are installed in a subdirectory called SPC. These files contain items (fonts, filters, symbols, and utilities) that can be shared with other Software Publishing products. That way, if you purchase another SPC Windows application, its Install program will not create multiple copies of the same data.

Unfortunately, this box is generic and doesn't reflect the path you entered at the beginning of installation. Regardless of what you specified, it will list C:\HGW as the path. On the positive side, it does tell you that "If you changed paths, yours will differ."

Starting Harvard Graphics for Windows

Once it's installed, follow these steps to load Harvard Graphics into your computer's memory:

1. Reboot your computer (press Ctrl+Alt+Del).

2. Start Windows.

3. If necessary, open the program group containing your Harvard Graphics icon. (To open a group, double-click on its icon in Program Manager.)

4. Double-click on the Harvard Graphics program icon.

Step 2

The User Interface

The term *user interface* refers to how you interact with a software program. In Harvard Graphics, you give commands by choosing icons and menu options, and by pressing function keys and Ctrl key-combinations; you can do this with both the mouse and the keyboard. Step 2 explains these various techniques. Before we get involved in the specifics of the user interface, however, let's examine a few Harvard Graphics terms and concepts.

Harvard Graphics Terms and Concepts

Slide is the term Harvard uses to refer to a chart. A slide can be a graph (such as a pie or bar), a text-only chart (such as a bulleted list or columnar table), an organization chart, or a drawing (such as a map). You can view the slides on screen, or you can produce printouts, 35-mm slides, or overhead transparencies.

Presentations

In the DOS version of Harvard Graphics, each chart is stored in a separate disk file. In the Windows version, related charts are grouped into a *presentation* and stored in a single file. For instance, to create a series of charts for a presentation to new employees, you create a new presentation file, and add a slide for each chart. Even when all you want to do is create a single chart, the procedure is the same: You create a presentation file and add the one slide.

Views

Harvard Graphics for Windows offers three ways to view your presentation. In *Slide Editor* view, you see a WYSIWYG (*What You See Is What You Get*) representation of a chart. This view is the one you use to enhance and modify the chart. You will work in Slide Editor view later in this Step.

Slide
Editor
view

*Slide
Sorter
view*

In *Slide Sorter* view, you see all the slides in your presentation. The presentation in Figure 2.1 shows miniature versions of ten charts in Slide Sorter view. Below each chart are a slide number and the first several characters of the chart's title.

*Outliner
view*

The third view, *Outliner*, shows the structure of your presentation in an outline format. Figure 2.2 is an example of a presentation in Outliner view.

Using Menus

If you have used other Windows applications, you already know how to use the menus in Harvard Graphics. To display a pull-down menu, simply click on the desired item in the menu bar. Or, with the keyboard, press Alt to activate the menu and then type the underlined letter of the item in the menu bar. (You don't have to hold Alt down as you press the letter.) Once a menu is pulled down, you can

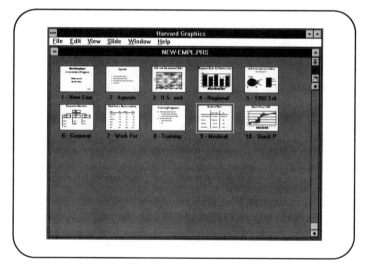

Figure 2.1: A presentation in Slide Sorter view

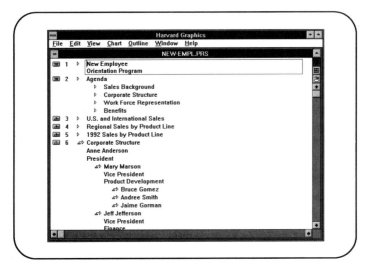

Figure 2.2: A presentation in Outliner view

select an option using one of the following methods:

- Click on it with the mouse.

- Use the arrow keys to highlight it and then press Enter.

- Type the underlined letter of the option.

Depending on which option you select, one of several things will happen. If the option has an ellipsis after it (as with Open... in the File menu), a dialog box will appear. If a ► symbol appears after the option (as with ScreenShow ► in the File menu), you will see a cascading menu of additional options. If the option has no symbol following it, the option will immediately perform its designated task.

Speed Keys

Some menu options offer shortcut keyboard equivalents, called *speed keys*. When a shortcut is available, it is listed next to the menu option. For example, on the File menu, Ctrl+O appears next to

Open. Thus, instead of opening a file by pulling down the File menu and choosing Open, you can simply press Ctrl+O. Once you have memorized the speed keys, you will find them to be a faster way of issuing commands.

Creating a Presentation

The charts you will create in this book are for a presentation to the new employees of a fictitious toy-manufacturing company called Tactile Toys. Ultimately, the charts will be made into overheads for the orientation program. In the process of preparing this presentation, you will learn all the chart types offered in Harvard Graphics.

The first slide in this presentation will be a *title chart*. Title charts are typically used as cover pages for reports or as introductory slides for presentations.

1.   Pull down the File menu by clicking on File in the menu bar. Or, using the keyboard, press Alt and type **F**.

2.   On the pull-down menu, choose New Presentation by clicking on the option; with the keyboard, you can press Enter (since the option is already highlighted) or type **N**.

3.   The Add Slide dialog box appears so that you can select the type of chart you want to add to the presentation. Title is already selected, so click on the OK button to create a title chart.

Filling in a Data Form

When you create a chart in Harvard Graphics, you'll work with a dialog box, called a *data form,* into which you enter the chart data (text and/or numbers). The layout of the form varies depending on the type of chart you are creating. In a title chart, for instance, there are three fields: Title, Subtitle, and Footnote. You can type as many lines as you like in each of these fields.

Moving the Cursor

Regardless of the chart type, follow these general rules to position the cursor (called "insertion point" in Windows) for data entry:

- Use the Enter key to move the cursor to the beginning of the next line.

- Press the ↑ key to move to the previous line.

- Use the Tab key to move to the next column or field.

- Press Shift+Tab to move to the previous column or field.

Using the keyboard

Mouse users can position the cursor by simply moving the mouse pointer to where you want the cursor to be, and clicking the left mouse button.

Using the mouse

Follow these steps to enter data into the title chart's data form:

1. To enlarge the data form, click on the Maximize button in the form's upper-right corner.

2. In the Title field, type **New Employee** and press Enter. The cursor moves down to the next line in the same field.

3. Type **Orientation Program** and press Tab. The cursor moves to the next field.

4. In the Subtitle field, type **Welcome to** and press Enter.

5. Type **Tactile Toys, Inc.** and press Tab.

6. In the Footnote field, type **Rev. 10/92**.

7. Choose OK to close the data form dialog box.

The data is now shown as a slide in the Slide Editor.

Working in Slide Editor View

You will work in Slide Editor view most of the time you are using Harvard Graphics. It is here that you will enhance your chart with special effects, format its text, annotate the chart, add clip art, and reposition *objects* (such as text blocks, the chart itself, shapes created with the drawing tools, and imported graphics).

Figure 2.3 illustrates the important areas of the Slide Editor window. The *view icons* on the right provide a quick way to switch to other views. The buttons at the bottom of the window let you go to or create other slides. The *toolbox* on the left contains icons you will select to create shapes (lines, boxes, circles, and so forth), manipulate objects, edit the data form, specify text and line attributes, and assign colors. The inside covers of this book contain descriptions of all of the tools. Refer to these descriptions as needed whenever the text in this book calls for you to use a tool.

Selecting
objects

Initially, the Selection tool is active. (To determine the active tool, look for the icon that is colored differently from the others.) You will use the Selection tool to select the object you want to format or manipulate. For example, suppose you want the title to be closer to the top of the slide. Before you can move this object, you must select it.

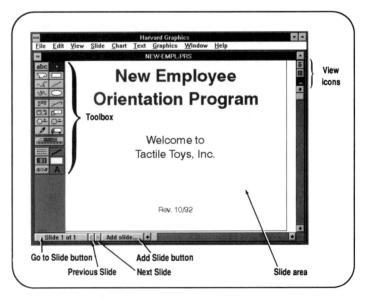

Figure 2.3: The Slide Editor view of a slide

1. With the Selection tool active, click the mouse pointer on the object you want to select (*New Employee Orientation Program*). Notice how this action places *selection handles* around the selected object. At this point, you can delete, move, copy, or format the object.

2. Make sure the mouse pointer is inside the selected object (the pointer will change shape to consist of four arrowheads.)

3. Click and hold the mouse button as you drag upward. A box that represents the size of the text moves in the same direction.

4. When the box is in the desired position (see Figure 2.3), release the mouse button. The text will then move into place.

5. To see a full-screen preview of the slide, press F2. (This is the speed key for Preview Slide on the View menu.)

6. Press any key or click a mouse button to return to the Slide Editor.

Managing Presentation Files

The commands for creating, saving, opening, and closing presentation files are located on the File menu. Use the Save As option to assign a new name to a file; use Save (or press Ctrl+S) to save the file with the same name. Presentation files are automatically assigned the filename extension .PRS.

In Harvard Graphics for Windows, you can have up to four presentations open simultaneously—you needn't close one file before opening another. This capability makes it easy to copy or move slides between presentations. When you have several files open, use the Window pull-down menu to display another presentation.

Follow these steps to save, close, and open the current presentation.

1. Pull down the File menu and choose Save As.

2. Next to the Filename text box, type **NEW-EMPL** and

press Enter. The file name, NEW-EMPL.PRS, appears in the window title bar.

3. To clear the presentation from memory, pull down the File menu and choose Close.

4. Now retrieve the presentation again. Pull down the File menu and choose Open.

5. In the Files list, double-click on NEW-EMPL.PRS.

Getting Help

Harvard Graphics has a comprehensive on-line Help facility that gives you instant information about any command, as well as explanations of many different topics. To display the Help index or find information about using the Help feature, use the Help pull-down menu. When you are in the process of invoking a command, or when a dialog box is displayed on screen, you can press F1 to display a help window specific to your current task. You can also place the mouse pointer on an icon or option and hold down the mouse button as you press F1.

When you have finished reading the help screens, close the Help window by choosing Exit on its File menu. Make sure you don't choose Exit on the Harvard Graphics File menu, or you will exit the program!

Witor's
GOLDEN POKER

Witor's
GOLDEN POKER

Witor's
GOLDEN POKER

Witor's
GOLDEN POKER

LATTE (cacao minimo 30%)
ALI.

ntero in polvere. Burro di cacao. Pasta
egetali, Nocciole, Latte magro in polvere,
.) Aromi, Emulsionante: lecitina di soia

ei Frati (CR) - Via Levata, 2 - Prodotto
14 - Sommacampagna (VR) - ITALIA

PRALINA DI CIOCCOLATO AL LATTE (cacao minimo 30%)
CON CREMA DI NOCCIOLA E CEREALI
Ingredienti: Esterno: Zucchero, Latte intero in polvere, Burro di cacao, Pasta
di cacao, Ripieno: Zucchero, Grassi vegetali, Nocciole, Latte magro in polvere,
Cacao magro, Cereali (frumento, mais). Aromi, Emulsionante: lecitina di soia
NUOVA WITOR S.r.l. - Corte dei Frati (CR) - Via Levata, 2 - Prodotto
nello stabilimento di via Industria, 14 - Sommacampagna (VR) - ITALIA

PRALINA DI CIOCCOLATO AL LATTE (cacao minimo 30%)
CON CREMA DI NOCCIOLA E CEREALI
Ingredienti: Esterno: Zucchero, Latte intero in polvere, Burro di cacao, Pasta
di cacao, Ripieno: Zucchero, Grassi vegetali, Nocciole, Latte magro in polvere,
Cacao magro, Cereali (frumento, mais). Aromi, Emulsionante: lecitina di soia
NUOVA WITOR'S S.r.l. - Corte dei Frati (CR) - Via Levata, 2 - Prodotto
nello stabilimento di via Industria, 14 - Sommacampagna (VR) - ITALIA

Step 3

Working with Text

In this Step, you will learn different ways to edit and enhance chart text. For example, you will see how to change fonts, italicize words, align a text block, choose a different color for a title, and add special effects. You will also learn how to correct mistakes, both manually and with the spelling checker.

Changing Text Attributes

Harvard Graphics lets you assign a variety of attributes to the text in your charts, as described in the following table.

Attribute	*Description*
Font	The typeface assigned to the text. Harvard Graphics comes with five soft fonts (Swiss, Swiss Thin, Dutch, GeoSlab and Monospace), but your system may offer additional typefaces.
Size	The size of the text, measured in points.
Color	Your color selections depend on which color palette you are using.
Style	Choose from bold, italic, strikethrough, and underline.

Attributes can be assigned to individual characters or to entire *text blocks* (such as the Title, Subtitle, and Footnote regions in a title chart). See the later section, "Formatting Characters," for a discussion of assigning attributes character by character. To format a text block, you select it and then use one of the following techniques to assign attributes:

- To change several attributes, pull down the Text menu and choose All Attributes. This displays the dialog box shown in Figure 3.1. A quicker way to display the Text Attributes

Changing attributes

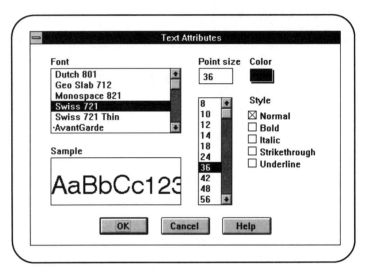

Figure 3.1: The Text Attributes dialog box

dialog box is to click on the Text Attributes tool. (See the inside covers of this book for a picture of this tool.)

- To change one attribute, pull down the Text menu and choose Font, Size, Color, or Style.

- To change the color of an object, click on the Fill tool (above the Text Attributes tool).

Here are a few tips for setting text attributes:

- If you are going to display the chart on an overhead or slide projector, make the text as large as possible so that people at the back of the room are able to see the chart clearly.

- Make sure the most important information in a text chart is larger than the other text.

- To avoid the "ransom note" look, use only one or two fonts per slide.

- Don't use too many different colors and styles in a chart—otherwise these special effects lose their impact.

In the following exercise, you will change text attributes in your title chart.

1. If necessary, open the NEW-EMPL.PRS file you created in Step 2.

2. Select the subtitle (*Welcome to...*) by clicking on the text.

3. Pull down the Text menu and choose All Attributes, or click on the Text Attributes tool.

4. In the Fonts list box, click on Dutch 801.

5. In the Point Size list box, choose 48 (or you can type **48** in the Point Size text box).

6. For the Style, mark the Bold check box.

7. Choose OK to close the dialog box and see the results of your formatting.

8. Select the title (*New Employee...*) and change the font to Dutch.

9. Select the footnote (*Rev. 10/92*) and reduce the size to 14 points.

Formatting Characters

In the previous exercise, you saw how to assign attributes to an entire text block. To change the attributes for specific lines or individual characters, you first need to use the Text tool to display the text in a *text box*, as shown in Figure 3.2. Actually, you can do a lot more in a text box besides format characters; you can type, edit, and align text, as well as set tabs and indents.

Let's change the company name (*Tactile Toys, Inc.*) in the title chart to italic.

1. Select the subtitle.

2. In the toolbox, click on the Text tool—the abc icon. The subtitle now appears in a text box.

3. Click-and-drag across the text *Tactile Toys, Inc.*

Figure 3.2: A text box

4.   Press Ctrl+I, the speed key for the italic style.

5.   To close the text box, click on the Selection tool.

Changing Colors

A presentation uses a *color palette* to determine the color of each element on a slide. For instance, a particular color palette may create yellow titles, blue subtitles, cyan x-axis labels, and bars in varying shades of green. However, you are not stuck with these color assignments. (You'll learn more about x-axis labels and other chart elements in later Steps.)

Custom colors

Harvard Graphics offers three ways to change the color of slide elements: You can choose a different color palette, modify the current palette, or assign a *Custom color* to a particular element. A Custom color is permanent and will not change if you apply a different color palette. For example, to change the color of the titles in all slides in a presentation, you would probably want to apply or modify a color palette (see Step 17 for details). To change the color of a title on a single slide, however, you should assign a Custom color.

Try this exercise to change the color of the presentation slide's title.

1. Select the title (*New Employee...*).

2. Pull down the Text menu and choose Color, or click on the Fill tool.

The resulting dialog box is divided into two sections. The top part, labeled Chart Colors, contains the current palette's colors for each area of the chart. The Custom colors are located in the bottom section.

3. In the Custom Colors section, double-click on the bright red color patch. The title is now colored red.

Adding Special Effects

Harvard Graphics offers several ready-made special effects that you can apply to text and other objects. To apply a special effect, use the Special Effects option on the Graphics menu and choose one of these effects:

Effect	*Description*
Frame	Encloses the object in a box
Drop Shadow	Places a copy of the object slightly below and to the right of the original
Sweep	Places a repeated sequence of the image (each one slightly smaller than the previous one) next to the original

Let's try creating a drop-shadow effect for the title, as follows:

1. If necessary, select the title.

2. Pull down the Graphics menu and select Special Effects.

3. Display the Effect drop-down list by clicking on the arrow. Choose Drop Shadow.

4. Click on the color patch to display the color palette.

5. In the Custom Colors section, select brick-red (below the bright-red patch) and choose OK.

Text Placement

In Step 2 you learned one way to position text, by using the click-and-drag technique to manually place the text block anywhere on the slide. Another way to position text is with the Justify option on the Text menu. With Justify, you can align text on the left or right, in the center, or spread it evenly across the line. Text is aligned within the boundary of the text block, as indicated by the selection handles. To align text within the slide boundary, use the Center on Slide option on the Graphics menu. This option centers an object on the slide, horizontally and/or vertically.

Here's how to right-align the footnote text.

1. Select the footnote.

2. Pull down the Text menu and choose Justify.

3. From the cascading menu, select Right. The footnote is aligned on the right side of the text block.

Editing Text

If you discover a mistake in your slide text, you can correct the error in the chart's data form or in a text box. You can then use the Edit menu to Cut, Copy, Paste, and Clear.

Follow the steps below to make some corrections in the title chart's data form.

1. To display the data form, pull down the Chart menu and choose Edit Data, or simply click on the Data Form tool.

2. In the Subtitle field, click-and-drag across the comma and the word *Inc.*

3. Press Del, or pull down the Edit menu and choose Clear.

4. In the Footnote field, change *Rev.* to *Revised.* (Place the cursor after the *v*, type **ised**, and delete the period by pressing the Del key.)

5. Choose OK to close the Data Form dialog box.

6. Press Ctrl-S to save the presentation.

Spelling Checker

It's a good idea to run your charts through the Harvard Graphics spelling checker so that you can catch any typos and spelling errors before you print. You can check a single chart or the entire presentation. The Check Spelling option is located on the Edit menu.

The spelling checker compares each word in your chart with an on-disk dictionary. When a word is not found in the dictionary, it is displayed in the Correct Spelling dialog box.

Adding words

- If the questionable word is correctly spelled after all, you can choose either the Ignore or Add to Dictionary button. The Ignore button skips over the word and goes on to the next questionable word. However, if you think you will use the word frequently in other charts, consider adding the word to the spelling checker dictionary. That way, the word will not be highlighted as misspelled the next time it is encountered.

- For real typos and spelling mistakes, select the correct word from the Suggestions list, or correct the word in the Replacement field. Then choose the Replace button.

The spelling checker does more than identify spelling errors. It also looks for irregular capitalization and repeated words.

Step 4

Bullet Charts

30

A *bullet chart* contains small symbols, called *bullets*, at the beginning of text lines in the chart. A variety of bullet shapes are available, including •, ■, ✓, and ►. Although this chart type automatically inserts the bullets, you can turn them off altogether if you want a simple list. Or you can create a numbered list.

You will begin this Step by adding a bullet slide to the new employee presentation.

Adding a Slide

To create additional slides in the current presentation, you click on the Add Slide button at the bottom of the Slide Editor window; you are then prompted for the chart (slide) type.

In addition to choosing a slide type, you have the opportunity to select a particular *chart style*. For example, in a bullet chart you can select the shape of the bullets, or in a pie chart you can choose two- or three-dimensional pies. To select a chart style, use the Chart Gallery button in the Add Slide dialog box.

The *Chart Gallery* displays on-screen examples of different variations of the chart type. Figure 4.1, for instance, shows the Gallery of bullet charts. Once you choose one of these variations, the options for that particular chart style are automatically set for you. Beginners will appreciate this feature because they don't need to experiment with options, struggling to achieve the look they want. Power users will enjoy the time saved by not having to manually set the options.

Chart Gallery

Follow these steps to choose a bullet chart style from the Chart Gallery:

1. If necessary, open the NEW-EMPL.PRS file.
2. Click on the Add Slide button at the bottom of the Slide Editor window.

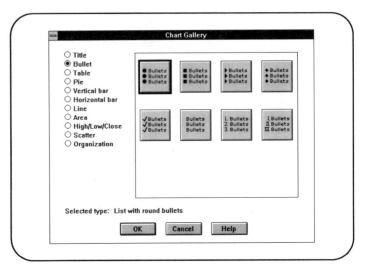

Figure 4.1: The Chart Gallery for bullet charts

3. From the list of slide types, choose Bullet.

4. Choose the Chart Gallery button.

5. Double-click on the style with diamond-shaped bullets. The bullet chart data form appears.

Entering Bullet Data

In a bullet chart, each line of text is automatically preceded by a bullet. In some of your charts, you may want multiple levels of bullets, with each level indented from the previous level. For example, the chart in Figure 4.2 contains two levels of bullets. To create an indented bullet, press the Tab key; press Shift+Tab to return to the previous level of indentation. You can create up to nine bullet levels.

Follow these steps to create the bullet chart shown in Figure 4.2:

1. Maximize the data form.

2. For the title, type **Training Programs**.

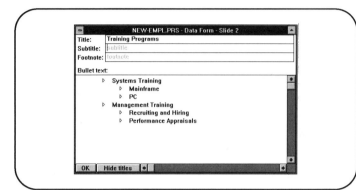

Figure 4.2: A bullet chart data form

3. Press Enter or Tab until the cursor is in the Bullet Text section. Notice that the bullet shape displayed in the data form is a right-pointing arrowhead; this is the standard symbol for the data form. You won't see the shape you selected in the Chart Gallery until you preview the chart or go to the Slide Editor.

4. Type **Systems Training** and press Enter.

5. Press Tab to create a second-level bullet.

6. Type **Mainframe** and press Enter. The cursor remains at the second bullet level.

7. Type **PC** and press Enter.

8. Press Shift+Tab to return to the first bullet level.

9. Finish typing the list, using the text from Figure 4.2.

10. When you're done, choose OK. The bullet list appears in the Slide Editor window.

Specifying Bullet Attributes

In the Bullet Attributes dialog box, you can change the shape, font, size, color, and placement of bullets in each level. This dialog box is displayed when you choose Set Bullet Attributes on the Text menu.

Let's look at the various options.

Changing the Bullet Shape

You may have noticed that the bullet shape you selected in the Chart Gallery applies to all levels. When you have multiple bullet levels, however, you will usually want a different shape for each level. In the upcoming exercise, you will change the second-level bullet shape.

Changing the Bullet's Font and Size

The Font option applies only if you select a number or letter for the bullet shape. For example, if you create a numbered list, you can select the font for the numbers. You can use the Size option to make your bullets larger or smaller.

Choosing a Bullet Color

To change the color of a bullet, click on the appropriate color patch. Then choose a Custom color from the palette. Note that choosing a bullet color does not affect the color of the text next to the bullet.

Adjusting the Bullet's Placement

The Distance option controls the amount of space between the bullet and the first character in the line of text.

To change the attributes of your chart's first- and second-level bullets, follow these steps:

1. Pull down the Text menu and choose Set Bullet Attributes. The dialog box that appears contains separate settings for each bullet level.

2. In the 1st Level row, double-click on the Distance field and type **.75**.

3. In the 2nd Level row, click on the current bullet shape (the diamond). The resulting Bullet Symbol dialog box displays the various symbols available.

4. Click on the first round bullet, and choose OK to return to the Bullet Attributes dialog box.

5. If you like, change the color of the first- and second-level bullets to blue. To do this, click on the color patch and then choose the blue patch in the Custom Colors section.

6. Choose OK to close the dialog box.

Editing Bullet Text

In Step 3 you learned about using the Edit menu to Cut, Copy, Paste, and Clear data in the data form or in a text box. These editing techniques apply to all chart types. With bullet charts, though, you have several additional techniques for editing data.

- To change the level of a bullet item, simply press Tab or Shift+Tab with the cursor anywhere on the affected line in the data form. For example, to change a second-level bullet to a first-level bullet, place the cursor on the line of the item to be changed, and press Shift+Tab.

- When you use the Cut and Paste commands to move a particular bullet item, Harvard Graphics automatically moves all of its sub-bullets—you do not need to select and move them.

- Instead of using Cut and Paste to move a bullet item, you can drag it to a new location. The following exercise demonstrates this technique.

Move the *Systems Training* section below the *Management Training* section.

1. Click on the Data Form tool, or pull down the Chart menu and choose Edit Data.

2. Click on the bullet next to *Systems Training* and hold down the mouse button; as you begin to drag the mouse, you will see a hand with a finger pointing to a horizontal line. This line shows where the text will be inserted.

3. Drag the finger downwards until the horizontal line is at the bullet's new location—at the bottom of the chart.

4. Release the mouse button.

5. Choose OK to close the data form dialog box.

6. Press F2 to preview your slide. It should look like Figure 4.3.

7. Press Ctrl+S to save the presentation with the same name.

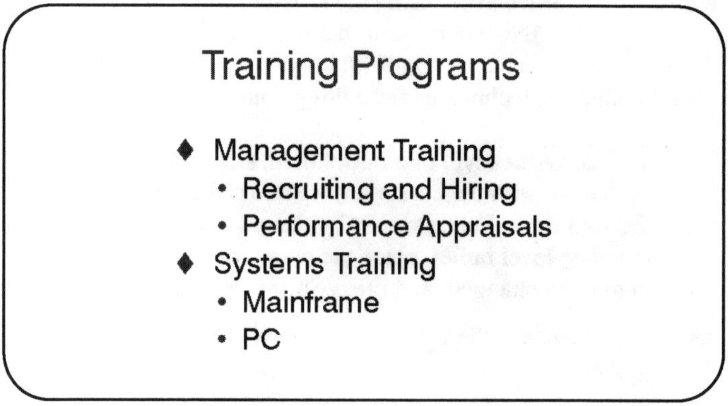

Training Programs

♦ Management Training
   • Recruiting and Hiring
   • Performance Appraisals
♦ Systems Training
   • Mainframe
   • PC

Figure 4.3: The revised bullet chart

A *table* is a text chart that displays its data in a columnar format—it looks something like a spreadsheet report you might produce in Lotus 1-2-3 or Excel, or perhaps like a tabular report you might create in your word processor. The Harvard Graphics table chart data form is actually very much like an electronic spreadsheet. When you create this chart type, you will work with a grid of rows and columns as shown in Figure 5.1; as in a spreadsheet program, the intersection of a row and a column in this grid is called a *cell*. The rows are numbered 1 through 2047, and the columns are labeled with letters A through Z and AA through AF. You can even perform calculations on the numbers in the cells, just as you can in a spreadsheet program.

Creating a Table Slide

The table chart you will create here has three columns; it compares major features of two medical plans. Follow these steps:

1. If necessary, open the NEW-EMPL.PRS presentation.

2. Since new slides are inserted after the current one, make sure the last slide in the presentation is displayed (look for Slide 2 of 2 in the button at the bottom of the window). If necessary, click on the Next Slide button (it looks like a > symbol).

3. Choose the Add Slide button.

4. From the list of slide types, choose Table.

5. Choose the Chart Gallery button. The Gallery displays sample tables with different combinations of horizontal and vertical grid lines.

6. Double-click on the style with horizontal and vertical lines after the first column and row (the first style). The table chart data form appears.

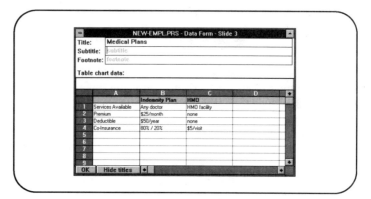

Figure 5.1: The table chart data form

Entering Data into the Table

The spreadsheet part of the data form contains a special area reserved for your table's column headings; this shaded row is located above row 1. You'll type the rest of your table data into the individual cells. Use Tab and Shift+Tab to move between columns, and Enter or the arrow keys to move between rows.

1.   Click on the Title field and type **Medical Plans**.

2.   In the shaded row above row 1, enter the column headings as shown in Figure 5.1. As you type, the text appears in the *Edit line* (under the heading Table Chart Data) not in the cells. Once you press Tab, the text appears in the cell, and the cursor moves to the next cell on the right.

3.   Starting in row 1, type the body of the table. The fastest way to type a table is to enter the data column by column, rather than row by row. That is, type the data for one cell, and then press Enter to move down to the next cell.

4.   Choose OK to close the dialog box.

As you can see, Harvard Graphics automatically created your table with well-spaced columns, aligned each item in the center of the cell, and placed *grid lines* after the first row and column (as per the style you selected in the Gallery).

Formatting the Table

There are a number of things you can do to improve the appearance of the table. For example, you may want to change the alignment of the text, specify a different style for the column headings, choose another text size or font, change the thickness of the grid lines, or alter the column widths. To format the table, you will use commands on the Chart and Graphics menus, as well as tools in the toolbox.

Selecting Parts of Table

Depending on what element of the table you are formatting, you may need to select the entire table, or a single row, column, or cell. Follow these rules to select areas of a table in Slide Editor View:

- The first time you click on table text, the entire table is selected.

- Once the table is selected, each subsequent click selects a different area, depending on where you click. If you click on the first cell in a column, that column will be selected. If you click on the first cell in a row, that row will be selected. If you click on a cell in the middle of a row or column, that individual cell will be selected. Keep clicking until the desired area is selected.

- To select multiple cells, hold down Shift as you click on each cell.

- To unselect an area, click outside of the table. (You may want to do this if you select the wrong area.)

In the following steps, you will format the text in the medical-plan table. In particular, you will reduce the size of the table text, left-align the items in the first column, and boldface the column headings.

1. To select the table, click anywhere on the table text. Selection handles should appear around the entire table.

2. Click on the Text Attributes tool.

3. In the Point Size field, type **20** and choose OK.

4. Click on the top cell in the first column (the blank cell). Selection handles will surround the first column only.

5. Choose Text, Justify, and then Left. The text in the first column is now left-aligned.

6. Click on the first cell in the first row. Selection handles will surround the first row only.

7. Press the Ctrl+B speed key to boldface the column headings.

Adjusting Column Widths

To adjust the width of a table's columns, select a column in the Slide Editor window (not in the data form). Then drag a selection handle to the left to narrow the column or to the right to widen it. You must drag one of the three handles on the right side of the column; the ones on the left will move the column.

Displaying a ruler

When setting column widths, it's a good idea to display a ruler to help you measure the columns. For example, if you want two columns to be the same width, the ruler provides an accurate way to accomplish this. To display the ruler, choose Ruler/Grid on the Graphics menu; turn on both the Show Ruler and the Show Position on Ruler options.

Modifying Table Grid Lines

When you added the table slide earlier in this Step, you used the Chart Gallery to select the table's grid line style (you chose a grid after the first row and column). If, after creating a table, you decide you want a different style or combination of grid lines, you can use the Grid Options dialog box. To display this dialog box, choose the Grid command on the Chart menu, or press F8 (the Chart Options speed key) and choose the Grid command button.

In Grid Options, you can turn on/off the display of the frame (an outline around the table), the row grid lines, and the column grid lines. Row grid lines can be placed after the first row only, after every row, or after a designated number of rows that you specify. Similar options are available for column grid lines.

Follow these steps to place grid lines after every column in your table:

1. Choose Chart, and then Grid.
2. Click on the Every Column option, and choose OK.

Specifying Line Attributes

Lines (such as the grid lines in the table) have several attributes you can adjust: color, thickness, and style (solid, dashed, and so forth). The attributes you set apply to all the grid lines in a table; you cannot select a 2-pt. thickness for the table frame and a 1-pt. width for the interior grid lines.

Change the color and thickness of the grid lines, as follows:

1. If necessary, select the entire table. (You may need to first click in an area of the window away from the table, to unselect the current table area.)
2. Click on the Line Attributes tool, or pull down the Graphics menu and choose Line Attributes.
3. For Thickness, choose 1 pt.
4. Click on the color patch to display the color palette.
5. Select the gray patch.
6. Choose OK to close the dialog box.
7. Press F2 to preview the table. Your table will look like Figure 5.2.
8. Press Ctrl+S to save the presentation with the same name.

Editing Table Data

In addition to the standard text editing options on the Edit menu
(Cut, Copy, Paste, and Clear), the table chart data form offers a number of editing operations on the Data pull-down menu. The Data
menu options, listed below, are similar to commands you would find
in a spreadsheet program.

Data Menu Option	*Action*
Edit cell data	Modifies the contents of the current cell
Go to cell	Moves the cursor to a specific cell
Insert	Inserts rows or columns
Delete	Deletes rows or columns
Fill right	Copies a cell to selected cells in a row
Fill down	Copies a cell to selected cells in a column

Medical Plans

	Indemnity Plan	HMO
Services Available	Any doctor	HMO facility
Premium	$25/month	none
Deductible	$50/year	none
Co-Insurance	80% / 20%	$5/visit

Figure 5.2: The formatted table chart

Step 6

Printing

This step explains how to get your charts onto paper—one slide per page, or several on a single sheet. Before you can print, though, you need to install your printer(s) in Windows 3.0. You may have done this during Windows Setup; if not, you can add printers at any time using the Control Panel. See your Microsoft Windows User's Guide for further information on installing printers.

Choosing a Target Printer

If you have installed Windows to use more than one printer, you'll first need to select the printer you want to use, your *target printer*. Because the target printer might influence the font choices you have in Harvard (since most printers have their own sets of resident type-faces), you should choose your target printer before assigning fonts.

To select your target printer, follow these steps:

1. Choose Setup from the File menu.

2. Display the Device drop-down list. These are the active printers installed in Windows.

3. Click on the desired printer.

That's all there is to selecting your target printer. However, don't close this dialog box yet—you may need to change some of your printer options.

There are a dizzying number of options for the several hundred printers that Windows supports. All of these options are accessible by clicking on the Setup Device button available in both the Setup and File Print dialog boxes. The specific options you have depend on your target printer. Click on the Setup Device button now to see the options you currently have available. Here are a few that are common to most printers:

Target printer options

Paper Size refers to the physical size of the paper on which you intend to print your charts.

Orientation lets you tell Harvard how to orient the on-screen and printed slide. A slide that is tall and thin is called *portrait;* a slide that is short and wide is called *landscape.* Most, if not all of your slides will be in landscape orientation.

Print quality

Graphics Resolution is the resolution, measured in dots per inch (dpi), at which your slide is printed. The more dots, the higher the print quality (and the longer the print time). For your rough drafts, you may want to save time by printing at a lower graphics resolution (say 75 dpi). Then you can switch to the highest resolution for your final printout. The Graphics Resolution option is available for Hewlett-Packard and many dot-matrix printers, but not PostScript printers, from which you get the highest possible resolution whether you want it or not.

Scaling is available for PostScript printers only. By entering a number here, you can define a percentage at which the slide is to be printed. At 100%, the slide prints at its actual size. At 50%, everything is reduced to half the actual size. If you enter a number larger than 100, the slide is enlarged.

Once you set an option in the Setup Device dialog box, it remains in force until you change it again. And we don't just mean in force in Harvard Graphics—the Setup Device dialog box is a pervasive Windows element that affects other open Windows applications, as well. For instance, suppose you set print scaling to 35 and then close Setup. If you then switch out of Harvard and into Word for Windows, and open Setup there, you'll see print scaling waiting for you at 35. You can see that it's a good idea to check your Setup Device options before you print, to make sure the settings still apply.

Print Settings

The options in the Setup dialog box shown in Figure 6.1 apply to all printing jobs in the current presentation. They can, however, be overridden for a particular print job, as will be discussed in the "Printing Slides and Handouts" section. Let's explore these printing options.

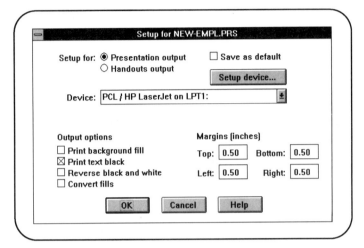

Figure 6.1: The Setup dialog box

Presentation or Handouts: Do you intend to print each slide on its own page, or do you want to produce thumbnails (miniature images) of your slides? If you choose Handouts Output, the dialog box displays a new option allowing you to specify how many thumbnail slides to place on each page. There are generally two reasons to print handouts: so you can give them to your audience, or to quickly print first drafts of your slides.

Print Background Fill: Background fill refers to the color or pattern of the slide's background. You will typically want to leave this option turned off when printing to your laser printer. Background fill patterns are complex and taxing on 300-dpi printers; they are best left for the high-resolution *imagesetters* (typesetting machines) and slide services.

Print Text Black: This handy option prints all text in black, even if the text appears in color on the screen. It does not convert the color of bullets, lines, or fills. If you use lots of gray scales or light colors for text, turning on this option will significantly improve the quality of your black-and-white output.

Mono-chrome printing

Reverse Black and White: Turn this on to reverse all black and white, and invert all other colors.

Convert Fills: When you are printing page proofs or printing to a laser printer, turn this option on to convert fill patterns to white. Processing the code required for fills, especially gradually changing ones, can send your laser printer to its knees; furthermore, at 300 dpi the results are often less than impressive. If your slides are destined for a high-resolution typesetting machine (imagesetter), your complex fill patterns will look glorious, but don't expect the same output from your laser.

Page margins

Margins: The only thing to keep in mind here is that your laser printer has a dead zone of between one-eighth and one-half inch around the outside of the page (depending upon the particular model).

Printing Slides and Handouts

Once you have determined that your print settings are correct, you are ready to print. Follow these steps to print slides or handouts:

1. Make sure your printer is turned on and has paper.

2. Choose Print on the File menu, or press Ctrl+P.

3. Select either Slides or Handouts.

4. Specify that you want to print all slides or a range of slides. If you choose Range, Harvard Graphics automatically enters the current slide number in the From and To fields; you can change these numbers as needed.

5. Change any options in the Print dialog box.

You'll notice that many of the options from the Setup dialog box are repeated here, allowing you to override the defaults for the current print job. Remember—the settings you made in the Setup dialog box are the default settings for the current presentation. The options here in the Print dialog box are for print jobs during the current session.

6. OK the dialog box.

Figure 6.2 shows a sample handout with four thumbnail slides on the page. (You'll create the fourth slide—the pie chart—in Step 7.)

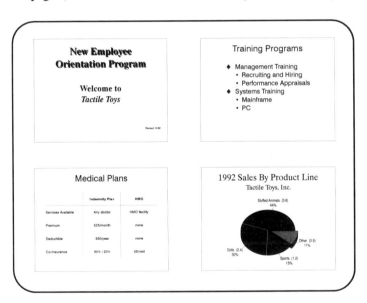

Figure 6.2: A printed handout

Step 7

Pie Charts

A *pie chart* is one of the most commonly used business charts. By looking at the relative size of the pie slices and their accompanying percentage figures, you can clearly see the relationship between several items.

In Step 7 you will build a three-dimensional pie chart that illustrates Tactile Toys's 1992 sales by product line, shown in Figure 7.1. Only the three major product lines have their own pie slice (Stuffed Animals, Dolls, and Sports); the other products are combined into a category called Other.

Although pies can have up to 24 slices, a chart with many small slices is difficult to read. For a more attractive chart, consider combining some of the smallest slices into a single slice labeled "Other" or "Miscellaneous."

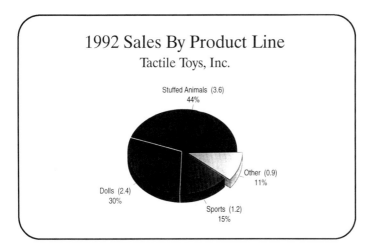

Figure 7.1: A three-dimensional pie chart

Choosing a Pie from the Gallery

To get a running start on your pie chart, you can choose a style from the Chart Gallery. As explained in Step 4, using the Chart Gallery is optional; it offers you the advantage of quickly selecting chart options by clicking on a sample chart.

Follow these steps to add a pie chart to the NEW-EMPL presentation:

1. If necessary, open the NEW-EMPL presentation file.

2. Click on the Next Slide (>) button at the bottom of the window until the last slide in the presentation appears.

3. Choose the Add Slide button.

4. From the list of slide types, choose Pie.

5. Choose the Chart Gallery button.

6. Click on the second sample chart—the single, three-dimensional pie. The description at the bottom of the dialog box reads *Selected type: 3D pie.*

7. Choose OK.

Entering Pie Chart Data

Pie charts use the same spreadsheet-like data form as table charts, except the pie data form indicates where to enter the labels and values for each pie (you can have up to six pies per chart). When you are creating a chart with a single pie, you need only enter data in the columns labeled Pie 1 Labels and Pie 1 Values. Type the descriptive text for each slice in the Labels column, and type the numeric data in the Values column.

Follow these steps to enter the data for your pie chart:

1. With the cursor in A1, type **Stuffed Animals** and press Enter. Notice that the cell displays *Stuffed Anim>* because the text is longer than the column width. You will learn how to widen the column later.

2. Refer to Figure 7.2, and finish filling in the spreadsheet. Don't forget to type the slide's title and subtitle at the top of the form.

3. To preview the slide, press F2.

Each slice is filled with a different color or shade, and is labeled with the text you entered on the data form. Below each slice label is a percentage-of-the-whole value that Harvard calculated from the values you entered. A line called a *slice pointer* connects each slice with its assigned label. This slide has a somewhat cramped appearance because the chart titles are too close to the Stuffed Animals label; we will fix this problem later.

4. Press any key to return to the data form.

Widening a Column

As you just saw with *Stuffed Animals*, when a label is too long for the current column width, the text is truncated and a > appears at the end of the text to let you know there are characters that aren't being

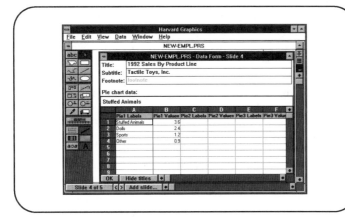

Figure 7.2: The pie chart data form

displayed. To widen a column, drag the column boundary to the desired width. This procedure is identical to the one used in Excel, 1-2-3 Release 2.3, and 1-2-3 for Windows.

Follow these steps to widen column A:

1. Place the mouse pointer in the spreadsheet frame, on the vertical line to the right of the column letter A. The pointer changes to a double-tipped arrow.

2. Click and hold the left mouse button.

3. With the mouse button held down, move the pointer to the right to expand the width. A dotted vertical line indicates the proposed new column width.

4. When the column is the desired width, release the mouse button.

5. Choose OK to close the data form.

Formatting Text

As far as text formatting goes, pie charts are no different from text charts: You can assign attributes (font, size, style, and color) to entire text blocks or to individual characters. To format the selected block, you can go directly to your Text menu or choose the Text Attributes tool. For further information on this topic, see Step 4.

In the following steps you will format the text in your pie. You will also move the pie down so that it doesn't crowd the chart titles.

1. Format the title in Dutch 801.

2. Format the subtitle in 36-point Dutch.

3. Click once on one of the slice labels (such as *Stuffed Animals*); this selects the entire pie. Click a second time, and the four labels (and their percentages) are selected. Change the size of the labels to 22 points.

4. To unselect the labels, click on an empty part of the slide.

5. Click anywhere on the pie; selection handles will appear around the main part of the chart.

6. The pointer is now a four-tipped arrow inside the selected pie; click-and-drag until the pie is positioned as shown in Figure 7.1.

Filling a Slice

Harvard automatically assigns each slice a different color. You can change these colors, or fill the slices with something other than a solid color. Pull down the Graphics menu and choose Fill; you will see the following choices on a cascading menu:

- *Solid* is the default fill.

- *Hatch/Pattern* fills the object with a crosshatch or pattern in the color of your choice.

- A *Gradient* fill contains two colors; it starts with one color that is gradually blended with another.

- *Bitmap* lets you import a bitmap image into the selected object. (A bitmap is a graphic that is composed of many tiny dots.)

Although Harvard lets you choose gradient and bitmap fills for pie slices, it's unlikely that you will want to get this fancy. These effects are more commonly used for slide backgrounds.

In the steps below, you will change the fill color of the *Dolls* slice.

1. Click inside the slice labeled *Dolls;* a single selection handle appears inside the slice. If you don't see the handle, click a second time.

2. Select the Fill tool; or choose Graphics, Fill, and then Solid.

3. In the Custom Colors section, choose the box in the last row, third from the right.

4. Choose OK.

If you don't like the default color assignments for the pie slices, you can edit the current color palette or choose another palette. See Step 17 for details.

Cutting a Slice

To cut, or *explode,* a slice from the rest of the pie, select the slice and drag it out of the pie.

Let's drag the *Other* slice away from the pie.

1. Click inside the slice labeled *Other.*
2. Place the mouse pointer on top of the selection handle. You will see a four-tipped arrow.
3. Click-and-drag the slice slightly out of the pie to the position shown in Figure 7.1.

Setting Pie Chart Options

All chart types, except Title and Bullet, offer a series of option dialog boxes for formatting the chart. You can display the main option box by pressing F8 or by choosing Chart Options on the Chart menu. This box contains several check box options and command buttons that access additional option dialog boxes, as indicated by the ellipsis (...) after the button name. The Pie Chart Options box is shown in Figure 7.3; notice that it has additional related dialog boxes for Series, Legend, and Labels.

After you designate options in any of the subsidiary dialog boxes, you are automatically returned to the chart's main option box. This organization is referred to as a *hub-and-spoke* system—the main option box is the hub and the subsidiary option boxes are the spokes. Each spoke is also available for direct access on the Chart menu.

In this section we will examine some of options you can set for pie charts.

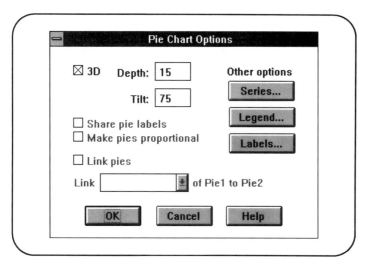

Figure 7.3: The options dialog box for pie charts

Setting Series Options

In the Series Options dialog box, you'll find options that can be set for each individual series. A *series* is a set of related data points. In a pie slide, for example, each pie is a different series; in an XY chart, you might have a series for each division of a company.

Our slide for Tactile Toys has only one pie, so any settings you change in the Series Options box will automatically affect this pie. If the slide had multiple pies, you would click on the appropriate pie number in the Edit list before changing any options.

The first slice in the data form begins at the three-o'clock position, and the other slices are placed around the pie in a counterclockwise direction, in the order they appear in the data form. The Series Options dialog box offers two choices for changing the order and position of the slices:

Rearranging the slices

- To arrange the slices from largest to smallest, turn on the Sort Slices option.

- To rotate the pie counterclockwise, enter a value between 0 and 360 (indicating degrees) in the Starting Angle field, or move the *angle indicator* on the dial. The starting angle, 0 degrees by default, is measured counterclockwise from the three-o'clock position in the angle dial.

Slice pointers

In the Slice Pointer drop-down list, you can select Short, Medium, and Long slice pointers (the default is Short). Or, if you don't want the pointers, choose None.

Column charts

Harvard Graphics offers a style of pie chart that looks nothing at all like a pie and isn't even round. Instead of arranging the chart data as slices in a pie, you can stack the data like a layer cake. Though not as commonly used as round pie charts, stacked column charts offer yet another way of comparing data.

Showing a Legend

The Legend Options dialog box lets you define pie slices with a single *legend* for the pie, instead of a label next to each slice. A legend lists each slice label with a corresponding color box. To use a legend, turn on the Show Legend check box in the Legend Options dialog box. You will also want to turn off the Show Slice Labels option in the Label Options dialog box, to prevent the slide from displaying duplicate information.

Labeling the Slices

The Label Options dialog box lets you choose whether to show the slice labels, values, and percentages. You can also tell Harvard where to position the values and percentages (below or adjacent to the label, or inside the pie slice), as well as how to format the numbers (using Currency and Decimal Places, for instance). The default arrangement is percentages displayed next to each slice label; this configuration works well for a typical pie chart.

When numbers and percentages are displayed inside the slices, it may be difficult to read them, depending on the colors you use in the pie. If you can't see a number in a particular slice, you can change the color used for that value. For instance, inside a dark-colored slice you may want the percent to appear in white; inside a light-colored slice, a black percent figure would be appropriate. To change the color of an individual percentage, click on it until selection handles appear around that number only. Then choose the Color command on the Text menu and pick the color you want.

Follow these steps to format the pie as shown in Figure 7.1:

1. Choose Chart and then Labels.

2. Click on Show Values to turn on this check box.

3. Choose Adjacent for the values.

4. Click on the Value Format button.

5. Next to Leading Text, type (. Watch the number next to Current Format: *(12345.123;* this shows you what the number will look like with the format you choose.

6. Next to Trailing Text, type).

7. Choose OK.

8. Click on the Percent Format button.

9. In the Decimal Places field, enter **0**.

10. Close the options dialog boxes, and press F2 to preview the slide. It should look like Figure 7.1.

Designing Charts with Multiple Pies

As mentioned earlier, you can have up to six pies in a single chart. You might want to place several pies on a single chart for comparison purposes—for instance, to compare sales data for two different years. Creating a chart with multiple pies is easy. The column headings in the data form indicate where to type the labels and values for each pie.

The Pie Chart Options dialog box contains several options that apply only if your chart has multiple pies.

Proportional pies

When you turn on the Make Pies Proportional option, Harvard totals the slice values in each pie and draws pies that are sized proportionally. For example, if the sum of the slices in Pie 1 is 200, and Pie 2's total is 400, then Pie 2 will be twice the size of Pie 1.

Linking two pies

When one pie is a detailed breakdown of a single "collective" slice in another pie, you will want to illustrate this relationship by *linking* the pies. Harvard then draws lines from the collective slice to the explanatory pie, so that you can clearly see the relationship between the two.

To link two pies, turn on the Link Pies check box in the Pie Chart Options dialog box. Then display the Link drop-down list and select the number of the slice to which you want to link the second pie. (Before you do this, you may need to take a peek at the chart data form to determine the slice number.)

Step 8

Bar, Line, & Other XY Charts

XY charts include any type of graph that is plotted on an x-axis and a y-axis: bar, line, area, high/low/close, and scatter. The unique aspects of each type of chart are discussed here in this Step; Step 9 covers the specific options for XY charts.

In this Step you will create a line chart that illustrates Tactile Toys's domestic (U.S.) and international sales for the period 1986 through 1991. Although the example used in this Step is a line chart, the procedure for creating other types of XY charts is similar.

The Anatomy of an XY Chart

Figure 8.1 illustrates the key components of an XY chart. Every type of XY chart contains the same key elements that you see in the line chart.

The horizontal axis at the bottom of the chart is the *x-axis*. In most graphs, labels appear on this axis, and usually these labels are units

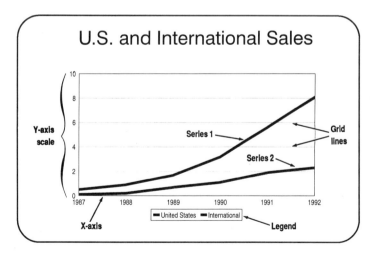

Figure 8.1: The key components of an XY chart

of time: years, months, quarters, and so on. The vertical axis at the left is the *y-axis;* it displays numbers on the *scale*. Harvard automatically determines an appropriate scale based on the numbers you enter in the data form. *Grid lines* extend from each value on the y-axis to help you read the specific data on the graph.

A *series* is a set of related *data points*. The graph in Figure 8.1 has two series (United States and International); Harvard can accommodate up to 16 series per XY chart. Whenever your XY chart has more than one series, it's important to have a *legend* that describes the data. Without the legend in Figure 8.1, you wouldn't know which line represents U.S. data and which one represents international sales.

Filling in an XY Data Form

The data form for the U.S. and International Sales line chart is shown in Figure 8.2. The first column is for the x-axis labels. You can enter these labels yourself, or have Harvard Graphics generate them for you (you'll learn how to do this shortly). The other columns initially are labeled with the series numbers (Series 1, Series 2, Series 3...) until you type over them with an appropriate description of the data in the series. These descriptions then become part of the legend.

Generating X-Axis Labels

Because the x-axis labels typically are evenly spaced units of time, Harvard offers a way to generate these labels automatically—with the X-Axis Labels button in the data form. All you have to do is specify the format (such as Month, Quarter, or Year), the start value and end value, and the increment. Harvard then fills in the X-Axis Labels column of the data form.

The *increment* is the number added to each start value until the end value is reached; 1 is the typical increment. For instance, if you wanted to create the labels 1980, 1985, 1990, 1995, and 2000, you would enter 5 as the increment.

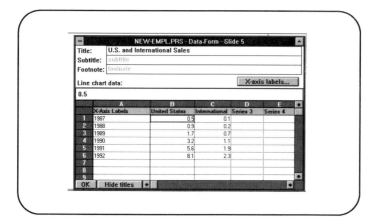

Figure 8.2: An XY chart data form

Creating a Line Chart

To see how all this works, follow these steps to create a line chart:

1. If necessary, open the NEW-EMPL presentation, and display the last slide in the Slide Editor.

2. Add a slide and choose Line for the slide type. In the Chart Gallery, select the first style, 2D Line.

3. Next to Title in the data form, type **U.S. and International Sales**.

4. To generate the x-axis labels automatically, click on the X-Axis Labels button.

5. In the Format list, choose Year.

6. Next to the Start field, type **1987** and press Tab.

7. Notice that Harvard has supplied its best guess for the end value (1991). You need to override this value, so enter **1992**.

8. The default increment, 1, is correct for this graph, so choose OK to close the dialog box. Column A is now filled with the years 1987 through 1992.

9. Enter the legend for the first series by typing **United States** over the *Series 1* cell at the top of column B. Type **International** for the second series legend. (You may want to widen the columns to see the legend text; use the technique explained in Step 7.)

10. Refer to Figure 8.2, and enter the data values shown there.

11. Choose OK. The line chart is now displayed in the Slide Editor.

12. Save the presentation with the same name.

Choosing an XY Chart Type

Determining which type of XY chart will best illustrate your data is not always a straightforward decision. Sometimes it's a trial-and-error process; you can try one chart type, and if it doesn't convey the right message or doesn't look just right, Harvard lets you easily try another type by using the Change Chart Type option on the Chart menu.

Line Charts

In a line chart, line segments connect each data point. Line charts are good for showing changes over time, for demonstrating a trend, and for showing a relationship between two or more series.

Bar Charts

There are two types of bar charts in the Add Slide dialog box: vertical and horizontal. Vertical bar charts, the most common, have a vertical y-axis and a horizontal x-axis. In a horizontal bar chart, the axes are reversed.

Area Charts

An area chart is a cross between a line and a bar chart. Like a line chart, lines connect each data point. Like a bar chart, fill colors or patterns represent each series. Area charts are typically used to show changes in volume over time. Figure 8.3 shows an area chart.

High/Low/Close Charts

The primary use for the high/low/close chart is to graph the fluctuations in stock prices. This chart type usually has four series: High, Low, Close, and Open. High is the stock's highest price of the time period, Low is the lowest price, Close is the final price at the end of the time period, and Open is the initial price at the beginning of the time period. The Close and Open series are optional.

Figure 8.4 is an example of this chart type. The high and low data points are connected to form a rectangular bar. The closing price is a horizontal line that crosses the right side of the bar, and the opening price line crosses on the left.

This chart type is not restricted to stock data. You can also graph other types of high/low data, such as temperatures, test scores, sales, and project bids.

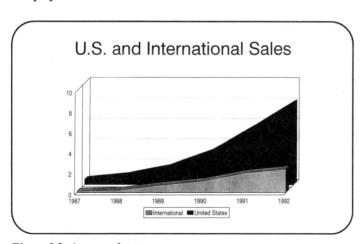

Figure 8.3: An area chart

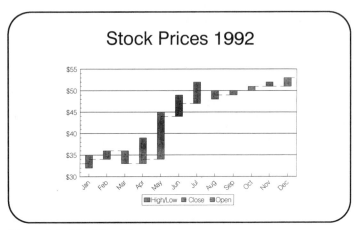

Figure 8.4: A high/low/close chart

Scatter Charts

A scatter chart is basically a line chart without the lines—only the data-point markers are displayed. Most often, the x-axis on a scatter chart contains numbers instead of time units. These charts are typically used to illustrate whether a correlation (relationship) exists between two independent variables.

XY charts have more options than any other chart type. In fact, there are six dialog boxes full of XY options, not including the main Chart Options box. We can't cover every single option here, so we'll concentrate on the ones you are most likely to use. If you are unsure of what a particular option does, click on the option as you press F1; the Help window will give you a brief explanation.

Figure 9.1 shows the main Chart Options dialog box for XY charts, and Table 9.1 briefly describes the main function of each of the option categories.

Category	Function
Series	Format characteristics of each series (color, marker style, line style)
Legend	Position legend, and format frame around legend
Frame	Select color and style for chart's frame
Grid	Turn on/off display of grid on x- and y-axes; select line style of grid
Axis	Enter title for x- and y-axes; format tick marks; scale axes
Labels	Format labels on x- and y-axes

Table 9.1: Option Categories for XY Charts

"Generic" Options

Some of the chart options apply to specific types of XY charts, and others work for all types. For details on these and many other chart-specific options, see "Options for Specific Chart Types" later in this Step. For now, let's concentrate on the "generic" options.

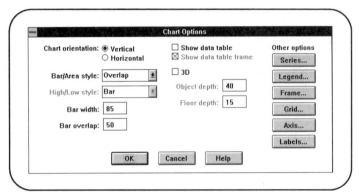

Figure 9.1: Chart Options dialog box for XY charts

Positioning the Legend

The default position of the legend depends on the chart type. On your line chart, the legend is at the bottom; on a vertical bar, the legend is on the right side of the slide; on a high/low/close chart, there is no legend. In the Legend Options dialog box you can choose a different position for the legend, place the legend inside or outside the chart frame, and select a style for the legend frame. You can also elect not to display the legend at all.

Continuing with the line chart you created in Step 8, follow these steps to move the legend inside the line chart's frame:

1. If necessary, open the NEW-EMPL presentation and go to the line slide.

2. Choose Chart, and then Legend.

3. For Location, click on the button at the 12:00 position.

4. For the placement, choose the Inside button.

5. For the frame style, choose Round Corners.

6. Close the dialog box. The legend is now centered inside the chart frame.

Formatting the Grid Lines

As you may have noticed, Harvard Graphics draws horizontal dotted lines from each value on the y-axis. These *grid lines* make it easier to read and understand the chart. The Grid Options dialog box lets you specify your grid-line style (such as dotted or dashed) for the x- and y-axes, or you can turn off the lines altogether.

To create solid grid lines or change their color, use the Line At-tributes tool.

Formatting the Axes

Both the Axis Options and Label Options dialog boxes give you options for formatting the x- and y-axes. You will want to go to the Label Options dialog box if your x-axis labels are crowded (you can slant them, place them vertically, or stagger them), or if you need to format the numbers on the y-axis (for example, with dollar signs or commas).

Use the Axis Options dialog box to add axis titles, format the tick marks, or change the scale. This dialog box, shown in Figure 9.2, has separate areas for each of the axes. The x-axis information is on the left, and the y-axes (Y1 and Y2) settings are on the right.

Identifying Data Values

When it's important to know the exact values associated with each data point on an XY chart, you can add a data table or data labels. A *data table* is a minispreadsheet of your values, placed at the bottom of the chart. To turn on this feature, choose the Show Data Table option in the main Chart Options dialog box.

Data tables

The *data label* feature places the chart's values near each data point. The Show Data Labels option is tucked away in the Label Options dialog box. Once you turn on this check box, you can se-lect the labels' position relative to the data points (Above, On, or Below), and their orientation (Horizontal, Vertical Up, or Vertical Down).

Data labels

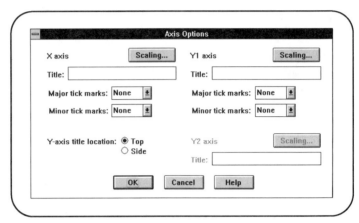

Figure 9.2: The Axis Options dialog box

Options for Specific Chart Types

In addition to the generic options that apply to all XY charts, Harvard Graphics offers some settings that work with specific types of charts. These chart-specific options are in the Chart Options and the Series Options dialog boxes. In this section, we will explore some of the options that apply to the various XY charts.

Line Chart Options

The Series Options dialog box contains a number of options applicable to line charts. Remember, each series can use different options—just click on the appropriate series name in the Edit list before you choose an option.

Choosing a Line Style

You can display your series lines with a variety of styles—solid (the default), dots, dashes, and a combination of dots and dashes. Note that these styles are available only in the hairline width (explained just below); if you want to use a different line style, you must first use the Line Attributes tool to choose a hairline thickness.

Selecting a Marker Style

You can place optional markers at each data point to identify each series. With the Marker Style option in the Series dialog box, you can select the symbol used for each series marker. Twelve different symbols are available. You may need to decrease the line thickness in order to see the markers.

Specifying a Line's Thickness

Although the various option boxes do not offer a way to change the thickness of a series line, the Line Attributes tool does. Just select the line and click on the Line Attributes tool, or choose this option from the Graphics menu. Line thickness is measured in points. The smallest width, which is called *hairline*, is less than a point wide; the largest width is 18 points. You can select one of the standard sizes (1, 2, 4, 6, or 12) or enter a size in the Other box.

Bar Chart Options

Using the Bar/Area Style option in the Chart Options dialog box, you can select a different style for your bar charts:

Bar chart styles

Style	Description
Clustered	Bars that correspond to each x-axis label are grouped together, side by side.
Overlapped	Part of one bar overlaps the adjacent bar.
Stacked	Bars for each x-axis label are stacked on top of one another.
100%	The y-axis is scaled from 0% to 100%, and the series are stacked.
Linked Stacked	Dotted lines connect the data points of each series in a stacked bar.
Linked 100%	Similar to the linked stacked style, except the scale ranges from 0% to 100%.
Horizontal Paired	Horizontal chart with two y-axis scales.

Some of these styles can be selected from the Chart Gallery when you add the slide.

Setting the
bar width

To create narrower or wider bars, enter a value (between 0 and 100) in the Bar Width field of the Chart Options dialog box. When you specify a smaller bar width, the chart will have more space between bars.

Area Chart Options

Three basic styles are available: stacked, overlapped, and 100%. These styles are similar to the ones available for bar charts. To change the style, select from the Bar/Area Style list box in the main Chart Options dialog box.

High/Low/Close Chart Options

High/low
styles

High/low/close charts come in three styles: bar, area, and error bar. To select the style, press F8 to get the main options box, and choose from the High/Low Style list.

The bar style, shown in Figure 8.4 of Step 8, is the most common type of high/low/close chart. The error bar style is similar to the bar style, except that a thin vertical line rather than a rectangular bar connects the high and low values. The area style shades the range between the high and low values, as well as the area between data points.

To adjust the width of the rectangular bars, use the Bar Width field in the Chart Options dialog box.

Scatter Chart Options

On scatter charts, you will frequently want to compare the data points to a particular line fit (such as a trend, average, or regression line). With the Line Fit options in the Series Options dialog box, you can tell Harvard to apply one of a variety of formulas to the data points in a series. The following formulas are available: Trend, Step, Average, Exponential, and Regression (Log and Power).

Step 10

Organization Charts

The most common use for an organization chart is to illustrate a corporation's structure. This chart, commonly referred to as an *org chart*, identifies the names and titles of the key players in a company or division (see Figure 10.1). Here are a few other ways to use organization charts:

- A regional structure of a company

- A simplified flowchart

- An outline of tasks in a project

- A family tree

- A diagram of a hard disk's directory structure

Before you create an org chart, you need to understand a few terms. At the top of the chart is the *top position*, such as the company president. Below the top position are several *managers*, and each manager may have one or more *subordinates*. In Figure 10.1, the subordinates of manager Jefferson are Andrews and Barret. Each

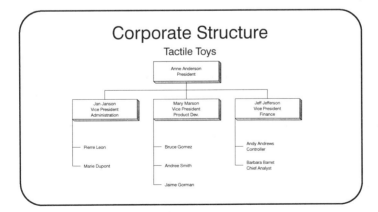

Figure 10.1: An organization chart

manager or subordinate can have two *staff positions*, such as secretaries and assistants. The staff positions appear as side branches of the main structure.

Creating an Organization Chart

In this chapter you will create an org chart that informs new employees about the corporate structure of Tactile Toys. Your final chart is shown in Figure 10.1.

1. If necessary, open the NEW-EMPL.PRS presentation.
2. To go to the last slide in the presentation, click on the Go To Slide button at the bottom of the window (the one that says Slide 1 of 5), type **5** and press Enter.
3. Add an organization slide.
4. Next to Title, type **Corporate Structure** and press Enter.
5. Next to Subtitle, type **Tactile Toys**.
6. Maximize the data form window.

Hiding the titles

7. To see even more organization text, you can temporarily hide the title area of the data form; click on the Hide Titles button at the bottom of the window.

Entering Data

Entering data in an organization chart data form is similar to data entry for a bullet chart. Just as you do in a bullet chart data form, you will use Tab to create a lower level, and Shift+Tab to raise the level.

Entering comments

Each item in the chart can have three pieces of information: name, job title, and a comment. For example, in Figure 10.1, *Jan Janson* is a name, *Vice President* is a job title, and *Administration* is a comment. As you can see on your screen right now, Harvard automatically gives you the fields for Name and Job Title. To enter a comment, however, you must issue the new-line command by pressing Ctrl+Enter. Also, use Ctrl+Enter when you need to enter multiple lines for the name field.

Let's start entering the org chart data:

1. For the top position's name, type **Anne Anderson** and press Enter.

2. For the job title, type **President** and press Enter. (Notice that Harvard automatically indents to get ready for the next item, without your having to press Tab. This is because there can be only one top position.)

3. For the first manager's name, type **Jan Janson** and press Enter.

4. For the job title, type **Vice President**, and press Ctrl+Enter to create a new line for a comment.

5. Type **Administration** and press Enter.

6. To create a subordinate for this manager, press Tab.

7. For the subordinate's name, type **Pierre Leon** and press Enter.

8. Pierre doesn't have a job title, so press Enter to skip over it.

9. Type **Marie Dupont** for the next subordinate's name, and press Enter twice. (She doesn't have a job title, either.)

10. Press Shift+Tab to enter another manager, **Mary Marson**.

11. Refer to Figure 10.2, and finish entering the org chart data. Remember the following as you enter the data:

    • Press Tab to create a subordinate (to go down one level).

    • Press Shift+Tab to create a manager (to go up one level).

    • Press Ctrl+Enter to enter a comment.

    • Press Enter to skip over the Job Title field.

12. Choose OK when you have completed the data form.

Preview your slide to see how it looks. Notice that the items in the first two levels are enclosed in boxes, but the last level is displayed vertically, without boxes.

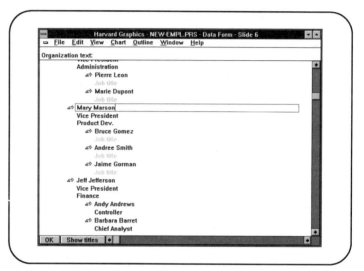

Figure 10.2: The organization chart data form

Formatting the Last Level

Currently, the names in the bottom level of your org chart are displayed with a vertical orientation. Alternatively, you can switch to a horizontal orientation, so that this level is presented in a format similar to the upper levels. To select the orientation for your chart's bottom level, choose Horizontal or Vertical in the Chart Options dialog box. You can also select the orientation from the Chart Gallery when you are adding the slide.

When there are many items on a horizontally oriented bottom level, the boxes will not only be very crowded, but the text inside will be difficult (if not impossible) to read. Therefore, for large org charts, you will usually want a vertical orientation for the bottom level.

Aligning Text

By default, text is centered inside each box. If you prefer to align the text on the left or right side of the box, you can change this alignment globally, using the text justification section of the Chart

Options dialog box. Note that the justification you choose here has no effect on vertically oriented text on the last level of the chart.

Preview your slide as it is now formatted, and study the text alignment of the last level. The subordinates for Jefferson look fine—each name and job title is centered on the tick mark next to the text. But the subordinates who don't have job titles are not properly aligned. Even though the job titles don't display, Harvard thinks they are there. Fixing this problem is a simple matter of telling Harvard to hide the job titles; then the names will appear centered next to each tick mark.

Hiding job titles

1. Display the data form by clicking on the Data Form tool.

2. Click-and-drag a selection box around the two names, Pierre Leon and Marie Dupont.

3. Choose Chart, Organization Charts, and then Hide Job Title.

4. Repeat steps 2 and 3 for the other names that don't have titles.

5. Preview the slide. Now, all the last-level names are properly aligned next to their respective tick marks.

6. Close the data form and save the presentation.

Formatting the Boxed Text

Harvard lets you change the font, style, and color of boxed text. You can't adjust the text size, because that's Harvard's responsibility. Harvard looks at the number of items on your chart and sizes the text accordingly, so that all the boxes can fit. If the text as such is too small to read, you may have to divide your chart into several smaller charts, using the Slide Summary feature in Outliner view.

Unlike the DOS version of Harvard Graphics, the Windows version does not have a command to format all the names, job titles, or comments with a certain style or color. For example, you cannot give a single command to boldface all the names. This task can be done in the Windows version, but you have to use the Text tool to format each name individually.

Formatting the Boxes

The Chart Options dialog box offers several styles for the boxes in your organization charts:

- Plain (rectangle)
- Rounded
- 3D
- Octagonal
- None

If you like, try some of the other box styles in the Tactile Toys org chart.

Restructuring an Organization Chart

Organizations change: People quit or get fired, hired, promoted, and, occasionally, demoted. Harvard Graphics makes the restructuring of an org chart a lot easier than the real-life equivalent. Table 10.1 briefly describes how you can modify an organization chart. This restructuring is done in the data form, not in the Slide Editor.

Task	*Action*
Demote an item	Press Tab.
Promote an item	Press Shift+Tab.
Insert an item	Place the cursor on the line above the new item and press Enter.
Delete an item	Select the characters and press Del.
Delete a manager and subordinates	Click on the manager's name, choose Edit and then Clear.
Move an item	Drag the icon at the left of the name into the new position.

Table 10.1: Commands for Modifying an Organization Chart

Step 11

Slide Sorter View

So far, you have been working exclusively in Slide Editor view—
the view in which you create your charts. But, as mentioned in Step 2,
Harvard Graphics for Windows offers two other views: Slide Sorter and Outliner. Here in this Step you will concentrate on Slide
Sorter view; Step 11 will explore the Outliner.

Slide Sorter view displays miniature versions of all the slides in
your presentation. Figure 11.1 shows your employee orientation
slides in Slide Sorter view. Notice that below each chart is its slide
number and the first several characters of the chart's title. Although
the slides are too small to show much detail, they are large enough
for you to identify the type of chart and its basic format. For
example, in Figure 11.1, you can easily see that Slide 4 contains a
pie, and that Slide 5 is a line graph.

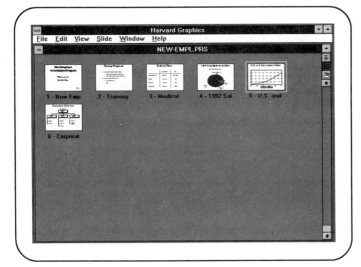

Figure 11.1: Employee orientation presentation in the Slide Sorter

Here are a few ways you can use Slide Sorter view:

- To get an overall picture of your presentation
- To help you locate a particular slide
- To place the slides in proper order for a ScreenShow (see Step 13)
- To copy slides to other presentations, as explained later in this Step

Viewing a Presentation in the Slide Sorter

The easiest way to switch to Slide Sorter view is to click on the appropriate view icon at the right side of the window. Or, from the View menu, choose Slide Sorter. The first time you go into this view during a work session, you'll need to have a bit of patience—the slides are drawn on the screen quite slowly. However, subsequent switches into the Slide Sorter will happen much more quickly, because Harvard remembers what the slides look like.

Follow these steps to practice switching between Slide Editor and Slide Sorter views.

1. If necessary, open the NEW-EMPL file. The first slide in the presentation is displayed in the Slide Editor.

2. Click on the Slide Sorter icon, and watch as the six slides in your presentation are slowly drawn on your screen.

3. To see a particular slide in more detail, click on it and press F2 to preview. Press any key to return to Slide Sorter view.

4. To display a slide in the Slide Editor (if you wanted to format or modify it), double-click on the slide.

5. Return to the Slide Sorter by clicking on its icon. Notice that this time Harvard draws the slides more quickly.

Zooming In and Out

Depending on the number of slides in your presentation, you may want to enlarge (*zoom in*) or reduce (*zoom out*) the size of the slides.

Figure 11.2 shows a zoomed-in presentation, and Figure 11.3 shows one that has been zoomed out. Notice that zooming in allows you to see more detail; zooming out allows you to see more slides at once. The Zoom command is located on the View menu.

Changing the Default View

When you create a new presentation or open an existing one, the default view is Slide Editor. However, you may want to open a presentation in Slide Sorter view, so that you can see your entire presentation and then determine which slides you want to edit or format.

The Preferences dialog box lets you specify which view is initially displayed when you open a file, and when you create a new presentation. (You can designate a different view for new and open presentations.) Preferences is an option on the File menu.

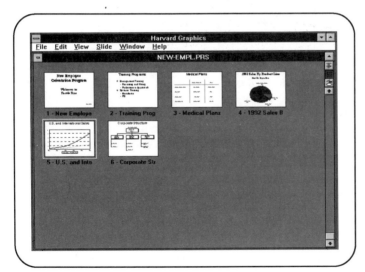

Figure 11.2: Zooming in enlarges each slide, allowing you to see more detail

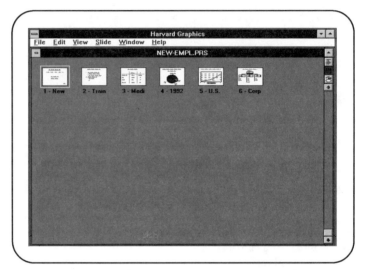

*Figure 11.3: Zooming out reduces each slide, allowing you to see more
slides at once*

Adding Slide Jackets

If your presentation doesn't have very many slides, consider adding
slide jackets, as shown in Figure 11.4. These jackets make the slides
resemble 35-mm slides. Be aware that you won't be able to see as
many slides at once, because the jackets take up additional space. To
see the jackets, display the Preferences dialog box and turn on the
Show Jackets in Slide Sorter check box.

Manipulating Slides

As its name implies, one of the Slide Sorter's main capabilities is to
sort, or organize, your slides. You can easily move, copy, and delete
slides using either the mouse or the keyboard.

Moving Slides

As you create slides in a presentation, you are probably not paying
much attention to the order of the slides. Most likely, you are

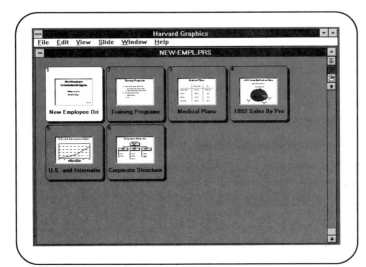

Figure 11.4: Slide jackets

concentrating on building and formatting each individual slide. Once they're done, however, you will want to reorganize the slides in an order that makes sense for the presentation. It is imperative that the slides are in the appropriate order when you are presenting a ScreenShow or printing handouts for your audience (see Step 13).

The fastest way to reorganize your slides is by dragging them to their new position in Slide Sorter view. As you drag the mouse, a tiny slide jacket appears. Place this jacket in the new location for the slide, and when you release the mouse button, the slide will move.

Copying Slides

If you want to create a slide that is similar to an existing one, don't start from scratch—instead make a copy of the existing slide and use it as a starting point. For example, at the end of your presentation you might want a summary slide that lists the same points as your agenda. Just use the Copy and Paste commands on the Slide Sorter's Edit menu to copy the agenda slide to the end of the presentation, and then modify its title in Slide Editor view.

Deleting Slides

If your presentation contains a slide you no longer need, delete it. To remove a slide, simply click on it and press Del (or use the Delete Slide command on the Slide menu). Deleting a slide is easy—perhaps too easy. Harvard does not ask you to confirm the deletion. As soon as you press the Del key, the slide disappears. Fortunately, you can use the Undo command (Alt+Backspace) if you accidentally delete a slide.

To delete several slides at once, hold down Shift as you click on each one. Each selected slide is enclosed in a border. When you press Del, all selected slides are deleted.

Copying Slides Between Presentations

Copying slides *between* presentation files is not too different from copying slides *within* a presentation. Here are the basic steps:

- Open both presentations, and switch to Slide Sorter view.

- Use the Window menu to select the presentation containing the slide you want to copy.

- Select the slide to copy and press Ctrl+Ins.

- Use the Window menu to display the other presentation.

- Click on the slide where you want the copy to go; the copy will be inserted after this slide.

- Press Shift+Ins to insert the copy.

Pasting a background

At this point, you may be presented with the Paste Background dialog box. In this box, you indicate whether you want to use the current presentation's background (which would abandon the background of the incoming slide) or rename the incoming background (which would leave the slide's background intact). In most instances, you will want to use the current presentation's background so that all slides have a consistent appearance.

Step 12

Outliner View

The third way to view slides in your presentation is in Outliner view. This view shows the structure of your presentation in an outline format. You see only the text suitable for an outline: slide titles, bullet chart lines, and org chart items. In Outliner view, you can perform the following tasks:

- Rearrange the slides
- Edit the chart data
- Enter bullet and org chart data
- Add slides
- Outline a presentation

You may notice some overlap among the functions available in Outliner and the other two views. For example, you can also re-arrange slides in the Slide Sorter, and you can enter data in Slide Editor as well as Outliner views.

Because you are working with text, as opposed to graphics, Outliner view is faster than Slide Sorter and Slide Editor views. You will never find yourself waiting for the screen to redraw. On the down-side, in the Outliner you may not be able to immediately identify each chart because you don't see a picture of it. (There are ways around this limitation, which you'll see shortly.)

Switching to Outliner View

To show the outline of your presentation, simply click on the Out-liner View icon on the right side of the window (or choose Outliner from the View menu). Figure 12.1 shows the employee orientation presentation in Outliner view.

Notice that the outline shows the slide number, slide title, bullet lines, and the items in an organization chart. Preceding each slide

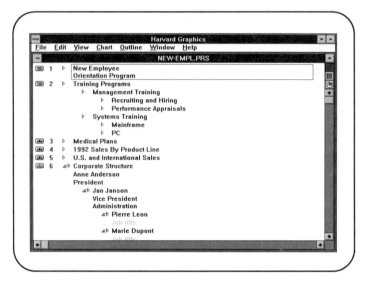

Figure 12.1: A presentation in Outliner view

number is an icon that indicates the general category of the slide:

Icon	Slide Type
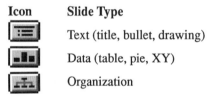	Text (title, bullet, drawing)
	Data (table, pie, XY)
	Organization

Follow these steps to show your employee orientation presentation in the Outliner:

1. If necessary, open the NEW-EMPL file.

2. Click on the Outliner View icon.

3. Use the vertical scroll bar to peruse the outline.

4. To preview a particular slide, click anywhere on the slide's text (such as the title) and press F2.

5. Press any key to return to the Outliner.

6. To display a particular slide in Slide Editor view, double-click on the slide icon (Data, Text, or Organization) in front of the slide number.

7. To return to the Outliner, choose the Outliner View icon.

Collapsing and Expanding the Outline

One of the advantages of working in Outliner view is that you can pick and choose which levels of the presentation to display. For example, you can display just the slide titles so that you can easily see the structure of the presentation. Figure 12.2 demonstrates this for your employee orientation presentation. Or, since organization charts have so many lines, you might want to temporarily hide the detail on these particular slides.

Hiding the details

Hiding certain levels of the outline is called *collapsing*. Redisplaying the hidden levels is called *expanding*. Collapse and Expand are options on the Outline pull-down menu.

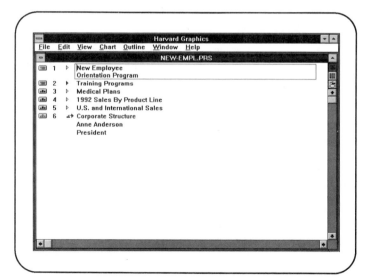

Figure 12.2: To display just the slide titles in your outline, use the Collapse option

The Collapse operation has two options: All to Titles, and Topic. The first option collapses all details of the outline, leaving you with just the slide titles (as in Figure 12.2). The Topic option hides the bullets or items underneath the current line—the line containing the text cursor. The Topic option lets you selectively hide different parts of the outline.

The Expand operation also has two options. The All option displays the complete outline, and the Topic option redisplays hidden bullets or items underneath the current level.

Let's practice collapsing and expanding your outline.

1. Click on the title for Slide 6 (*Corporate Structure*).

2. Choose Outline, Collapse, and then Topic. When you collapse an org chart, you see the slide title and the top position (*Anne Anderson, President*). Notice that the symbol next to the title is filled in (with blue on a color monitor) to let you know there are hidden levels.

3. To redisplay the detail for this slide, choose Outline, Expand, and then Topic.

4. To show only the slide titles in the outline, choose Outline, Collapse, and then All to Titles. Your screen will look like Figure 12.2.

Another way to collapse or expand a topic is with the mouse. Double-click on the bullet icon next to the slide title (this action is a toggle).

Modifying the Outline

Remember back to Steps 4 and 10 when you edited bullet and organization charts. Most of these same techniques can be used in Outliner view. In this section you will learn how to edit data, move bullet items, and rearrange the order of the slides.

Editing Data

You don't need to switch into Slide Editor view to edit the data in a slide. If the text is shown in the Outliner, you can edit it directly. So, to change a slide title, or the text in a bullet or org chart, you can simply make the correction on the outline. But in Outliner view you can do more than insert and delete text.

- To reorder bullet or org chart items, you can use the same techniques available in the data form: cut-and-paste or click-and-drag.

- To add another bullet or item, place the cursor on the line above where you want the new item, and press Enter. Harvard automatically displays a new line at the same level of indentation.

- To change the indent level, press Tab or Shift+Tab.

Moving bullet items

Obviously, editing data charts in Outliner view requires a different technique, since the data is not shown in the outline. To edit tables, pies, and XY charts, use the Edit Data command on the Chart menu. This command will overlay the data form on top of the outline.

Rearranging Slides

In Outliner view, rearranging the order of the slides in your presentation is similar to moving bullet or org chart items. Just click on the symbol right next to the slide title and drag up or down. You will see a horizontal line that represents the insertion point of the slide. As soon as you release the mouse button, the slide moves into its new location.

Outlining a Presentation

One approach to creating a presentation is to add slides, one at a time, in the Slide Editor. With this method, you concentrate on individual slides, rather than on the overall presentation. An alternative approach is to begin by outlining the structure of your presentation. In the Outliner, you can enter all your slide titles and then go back and fill in the chart data; this entails creating slides in Outliner view.

Here's how you might go about outlining a presentation:

1.   Change the default view for new presentations to Outliner view; you'll do this in the Preferences dialog box.

2.   Create a new presentation.

3.   Because you changed the default view, you are automatically in the Outliner. Type titles that describe the contents of each slide. If you prefer, you can also enter the items for the bullet charts at this stage.

4.   When you're ready to enter data for the charts, use the Add Chart to Slide option on the Chart menu. (This step is not necessary for bullet charts.)

5.   To customize the format of the charts, switch to Slide Editor view.

With the Harvard Graphics ScreenShow feature, you won't need to create overhead transparencies or 35-mm slides for your presentation—you can display the charts right on the computer screen, one after the other. Of course, for a large audience, you'll want to project the images on a big screen.

If you have created a set of slides in a presentation file, then you already have the ingredients for a ScreenShow. Using Harvard, you can determine the order in which slides are to appear, how one slide changes to the next, and, for fully automated presentations, how long each slide is to be displayed.

Viewing a ScreenShow

In the DOS versions of Harvard Graphics, you have to manually assemble a presentation. In the Windows version, slides are automatically grouped into a presentation, and to view them as a collection you need only issue one command. Try it:

1. If necessary, open the NEW-EMPL file.

2. To start the ScreenShow, choose File, ScreenShow, and then From Beginning. Or you can press the speed key, Ctrl+F2.

3. To view the next slide, press any key. When the Screen-Show is finished, the Slide Editor window appears.

If you need to change the order of the slides in your show, switch to Slide Sorter view and drag the slides into their new location.

Navigating a ScreenShow

Harvard provides many controls that enable you to move through a ScreenShow. The simplest way is to use the right and left mouse buttons to move forward and backward one slide at a time. This is especially convenient because you do not need to be next to your computer, and it doesn't matter where the mouse cursor is when you click. It's just like using the remote control on a slide projector. Other handy navigation controls include the following:

Home	Moves to first slide
End	Moves to last slide
Backspace	Shows previous slide
Esc	Stops ScreenShow
Any other key	Shows next slide

On your own, use these keystrokes to navigate through the NEW-EMPL presentation.

To start a presentation at a specific slide, the easiest course of action is to use the Go to Slide button to move to the desired slide, and then use the Alt+F2 speed key to display the presentation from there.

Setting Transition Effects

Now the fun begins! With the *transition effects* that Harvard Graphics offers for ScreenShows, you can create lively and professional presentations. These transitions define how a slide is drawn on the screen and how it is erased. For example, you can gradually fade a slide as it is erased from the screen, or open the slide up like a blossoming flower. Though you have the opportunity to go wild here, be careful—you don't want to make your audience dizzy!

Draw and Erase Effects

Figure 13.1 shows the Edit ScreenShow Effects dialog box. This box is displayed when you choose File, ScreenShow, and then Edit ScreenShow Effects. Here is where you determine how Harvard draws and erases slides on the screen. The Slide List box shows the six slides that make up this presentation, and if you click on each one, you will notice that the Draw Effect and Erase Effect boxes indicate *Default* in each case. This means, of course, that the standard settings govern the transitions for each slide. But what are those standard settings? To find out, click on the first item in the Slide List, Default Transition Effect. Now the two Effect boxes read

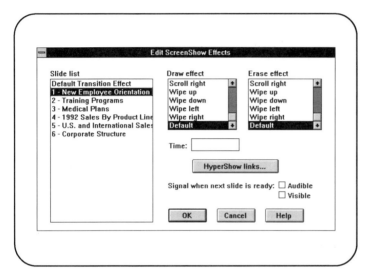

Figure 13.1: The Edit ScreenShow Effects dialog box

Replace and None, indicating that each slide will completely re-place the previous one, and there is no special erase effect—each slide will be erased with the draw effect of the next slide.

Most of the time, you will find the default transition effects to be adequate, but occasionally a bit more drama or excitement is in order. Let's try changing the transition so that each new slide rolls up quickly from the bottom.

1. Choose File, ScreenShow, and then Edit ScreenShow Effects.

2. In the Slide List, click on *Default Transition Effect.*

3. In the Draw Effect box, choose Wipe Up. That is all that is necessary to apply this change to all six slides, because they are all currently assigned to the default draw effect, and you just changed the default.

4. OK this box, and press Ctrl+F2 to run the slide show. To see each slide roll up (or "wipe up") from the bottom, press a key or the right mouse button.

5. Return to the Edit ScreenShow Effects dialog box and click on Default Transition Effect.

6. For the draw effect, choose Open Horizontal.

7. For the erase effect, choose Close Horizontal.

8. OK the box and run the show again. These two effects give the appearance of curtains opening and closing on a stage.

Customizing Your Presentation

The slides in a well-conceived presentation have a consistent appearance, and that is the value of setting a default transition effect—it enables you to establish a standard format for your presentation. It is equally valuable, however, to be able to single out a particular slide and treat it differently. The Edit ScreenShow Effects dialog box gives you this flexibility.

For example, let's add a special transition effect for the first slide in the presentation.

1. Open the Edit ScreenShow Effects dialog box.

2. In the Slide List, click on Slide 1.

3. Change the draw effect to Fade. Leave the erase effect set to Default.

4. Choose OK.

5. Run the ScreenShow and observe the fade draw effect on Slide 1.

6. Press Esc to cancel the show.

Automating the ScreenShow

Harvard Graphics offers a way to create a self-running presentation that doesn't require a keystroke or button click to display the next slide in the ScreenShow. You can set a default time interval for displaying all slides in the show; or, to display a single slide for a longer or shorter period, you can change the delay for that individual slide. Here's how to automate your ScreenShow:

1. Open the Edit ScreenShow Effects dialog box, and click on Default Transition Effect in the Slide List.

2. In the Time box, enter the number of seconds you want to display each slide. Or, to enter an interval in minutes and seconds, use the syntax *mm:ss*. For example, to display each slide for 2 minutes and 20 seconds, enter 2:20.

3. To change the delay for a particular slide, click on the desired slide in the Slide List and enter an appropriate value in the Time box.

4. OK the box and start the ScreenShow.

Setting a time value

Each slide displays for the specified amount of time, and subsequent slides will automatically appear—without your having to lift a finger.

If, during the ScreenShow, you want to display a slide for less time than you have programmed, you can press any key or the right mouse button to override the time delay and move the show along. However, there is no way to pause the presentation.

Creating a HyperShow

So far, you have worked with slide shows that are sequential: that is, Slide 4 follows Slide 3 and precedes Slide 5. Each slide appears in numerical sequence. The *HyperShow* feature throws such conventions out the electronic window. With HyperShow, you can do the following:

*   Create a slide show that will display slides in any order.

*   Build a menu-driven show.

*   Create user-friendly, on-screen prompts or *buttons* that jump to another slide when you click on them during a ScreenShow. A button is usually boxed text, though it can be any object on the slide.

Jump buttons

• Launch other applications (such as your spreadsheet program or word processor) from within a ScreenShow.

To create a HyperShow, you program a key or button to perform a certain action when it is pressed or clicked on during a ScreenShow. For example, you can program the Home key to display a slide containing the presentation's agenda. And don't let the term *program* scare you off—programming a HyperShow key is a simple matter of filling in a dialog box. Let's try it:

1. Open the Edit ScreenShow Effects dialog box.

2. If you want the HyperShow key to be available from all slides in the ScreenShow, click on Default Transition Effect in the Slide List. Otherwise, click on the appropriate slide number.

3. Choose the HyperShow Links button. The dialog box shown in Figure 13.2 appears.

4. Select a key from the Key/Button drop-down list.

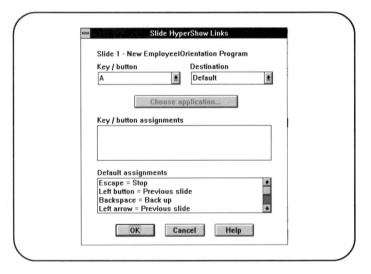

Figure 13.2: The Slide HyperShow Links dialog box

5. From the Destination list, select the destination (the slide you want to appear when the HyperShow key is pressed during a ScreenShow).

6. Repeat steps 4 and 5 for each key you want to program.

7. Close all the dialog boxes.

HyperShow is an extremely powerful feature, and we have only skimmed the surface of its capabilities in this Step. To discover more about this feature, refer to the documentation that came with Harvard Graphics for Windows.

Built into Slide Editor view are tools commonly found in drawing programs. You can draw a wide variety of shapes (rectangles, circles, lines, and so forth), type text anywhere on the slide, rotate and flip objects, and add clip-art pictures (called *symbols*). With these drawing tools, you can annotate your graphs—for example, you can explain an unusually high or low data point on an XY chart. You can also design custom drawings (maps, advertisements, logos, invitations, and so on).

The Tools

The tools for drawing objects are located in the toolbox on the left side of the window in Slide Editor view. Table 14.1 defines the drawing tool icons; you will learn more about each tool in this Step.

Tool Icon	Name	Description
	Ellipse	Draw circles and ovals
	Freehand	Draw freehand (as with a pen or pencil)
	Line	Draw lines and arrows
	Polygon	Create a closed object, with a variable number of sides
	Rounded Polygon	Create a closed, curved object
	Rectangle	Draw squares and rectangles
	Rounded Rectangle	Draw squares and rectangles with rounded corners
	Polyline	Draw two or more connected line segments

Table 14.1: Drawing Tools

Tool Icon	Name	Description
~~	Polycurve	Draw arcs and other open curved shapes
abc	Text	Type new text or edit existing text

Table 14.1: Drawing Tools (continued)

Pop-up tools

Note that some of the tools in the toolbox are actually two tools in one. If you click and hold on a tool, a related tool may pop up. For example, if you click and hold on the Rectangle tool, you will also see the Rounded Rectangle tool. The two-in-one drawing tools are

Main Tool	Pop-Up Tool
Rectangle	Rounded Rectangle
Polygon	Rounded Polygon
Polyline	Polycurve

If you will be using the drawing tools to annotate an existing chart, you can simply display the slide and start drawing. To create a drawing from scratch, select the Drawing slide type in the Add Slide dialog box. The Drawing slide type is actually a title slide, except that you bypass the data form and are immediately taken into the Slide Editor. But you can still use the Data Form tool to enter a title, subtitle, and footnote for your drawing, if you desire.

Follow these steps to create a drawing slide in a new presentation:

1. Choose File and then New.

2. In the Add Slide dialog box, choose Drawing for the slide type and click on OK.

3. Save the presentation with the name, PLAY.

The slide is immediately shown in the Slide Editor, and the only thing on the slide is the ghosted text, *Title*. (If this bothers you, you can click on the text and delete it. Either way, it won't print or appear in a ScreenShow.)

As you read this Step, use this slide as a drawing pad for practicing with the drawing tools. If you want to delete an object you create, just select it and press Del. To move a selected object, drag it to a new location. Feel free to play here. In Step 15, you will get to use these tools in a more meaningful way.

Using Tool Lock

The Graphics menu has an option called Tool Lock that controls what happens after you finish using a drawing tool. If Tool Lock is turned on, you are locked into that drawing tool; after you finish drawing an object, that same tool is automatically selected so you can instantly draw another object. If Tool Lock is turned off, the Selection tool is automatically selected after you draw an object. That way, once you've drawn something, you can either choose another tool or perform one of the Selection tool operations (such as moving, sizing, or formatting objects).

To see whether Tool Lock is on now, pull down the Graphics menu. If a check mark appears next to Tool Lock, it is on. This option is a toggle—use the same command to turn it on and off. We generally prefer working with Tool Lock turned off except in special circumstances—such as when we are drawing several rectangles in a row.

Formatting Objects

In previous Steps, you learned how to use the Fill and Line Attributes tools to format elements on your charts. The objects you create with the drawing tools can be formatted in a similar fashion. This next section summarizes these formatting techniques.

You can specify the attributes either before or after you draw the shape; if you are formatting after the fact, just make sure the object is selected.

Fill 'er Up

All closed objects (ellipses, rectangles, and polygons) are automatically filled with the current fill color. (To see what this color is, look at the color patch next to the Fill tool.) It's entirely likely that this color is not appropriate, or that you may not want any color at all.

You can change the fill color before or after you draw the object. Just click on the Fill tool (or the color patch next to it) and select the desired color; or, to create an object without a fill, choose None in the Custom Colors section.

Specifying Line Attributes

With the Line Attributes tool or the Line Attributes option on the Graphics menu, you can format the following characteristics of lines and object outlines:

- Thickness
- Style (dotted, dashed, etc.)
- Color

Creating Objects

If you have used drawing tools in other programs, you can probably figure out how to use Harvard's tools on your own. Otherwise, read through this section to discover the techniques for using each tool. Figure 14.1 shows various objects that were created with the drawing tools.

Typing with the Text Tool

The Text tool will be no stranger to you—you used it in Step 3 to format text. When you choose this tool with a text block selected, that text appears in a text box. At this point, you can format characters, correct mistakes, or type additional text.

Text annotations

This tool has a second function: You can use it to add text anywhere on the slide. Text that is typed directly on a slide is called an *annotation*. There are two ways to open a text box for new text.

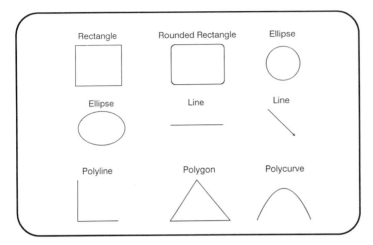

Figure 14.1: Objects drawn with the drawing tools

- Choose the Text tool, and then click on the slide where you want to add the text.

- Choose the Text tool, and then click-and-drag a box that has the approximate dimensions of the new text block.

Drawing Rectangles

Harvard Graphics offers two tools that draw rectangular shapes: one for sharp-angled corners and one for rounded corners. Drawing a rectangle is easy:

1. Choose the Rectangle or Rounded Rectangle tool.

2. Place the pointer where you want the upper-left corner of the rectangle to be.

3. Click-and-drag until the rectangle has the desired dimensions. To create a perfect square, hold down Shift as you drag.

4. Release the mouse button.

Drawing Circles and Ovals

Drawing an ellipse is exactly like drawing a rectangle—you just select the Ellipse tool, point, and click-and-drag. If you hold down Shift as you drag, you will create a perfect circle. (Be sure to hold down Shift when you size the circle, as well.)

Creating Lines and Arrows

To draw a line,

1.   Choose the Line tool.

2.   Place the pointer where you want the line to start, and click.

3.   Move the pointer to where you want the line to end. If the line is jagged as you are drawing it, hold down Shift to straighten the line. The Shift key rotates the line to the nearest 45° angle.

4.   Click at the end of the line.

Arrowheads

Harvard doesn't offer an Arrow tool, but it's easy to create an arrow—you just draw a line and specify an option in the Line Attributes dialog box. This dialog box has two options for specifying arrowheads: First Ending and Last Ending. With these you can choose either a small or large arrowhead for the beginning and/or end of the line.

The size of the arrowhead is proportional to the thickness of the line. For instance, an arrowhead on a hairline is barely noticeable.

Drawing Polygons

A polygon is a closed shape consisting of three or more points; polygons include triangles, pentagons, trapezoids, octagons, and so on. The Rounded Polygon tool draws these same shapes, except with smoothed curves instead of sharp angles. To create a polygon,

1.   Choose either the Polygon or Rounded Polygon tool.

2.   Click at each point of the polygon. Each time you click, the points are connected with a line. Notice that a dotted

line connects the first and the last point, representing the last side of the polygon.

3. When you're finished, double-click the left mouse button or click the right mouse button once. Harvard automatically replaces the dotted line with a solid one so that the shape is completely closed.

Creating Connected Line Segments

To draw two or more connected line segments, use the Polyline tool, which is quite similar to the Polygon tool. Both tools produce a series of connected line segments—the only difference is that the Polyline tool does not automatically connect the first and last points to create a closed object.

Polyline tool

To create several connected line segments,

1. Choose the Polyline tool.

2. Click at the beginning of the first line segment.

3. Click at the end of each line segment (which is also the beginning of the next line). Each time you click, the points are connected with a line.

4. At the end of the last line segment, double-click the left mouse button or click the right mouse button once.

Creating Arcs

The primary use for the Polycurve tool is to create arcs. Here's how to create an arc:

Polycurve tool

1. Choose the Polycurve tool (a pop-up tool of the Polyline tool).

2. Click at the beginning of the arc.

3. Click at the peak of the arc.

4. Double-click at the end of the arc.

Using the Freehand Tool

The Freehand tool lets you use your mouse as you would a pencil on paper. As you drag the mouse, a line traces the mouse pointer's path. (It's kind of like an Etch-a-Sketch.) Use this tool to draw designs and shapes that can't be produced with any of the other tools.

Step 15

Annotating a Chart

15

In this Step, you will use the drawing tools to annotate a data point on the line graph you created in Step 8. The annotated chart is shown in Figure 15.1. Three tools were used to create the annotation: Text, Ellipse, and Line.

Creating the Text Annotation

As explained in Step 14, to type text anywhere on the slide, use the Text tool and then either click on the slide or click-and-drag a text box.

To create the text annotation, follow these steps:

1. Open the NEW-EMPL file.
2. Go to Slide 5, in Slide Editor view.
3. If necessary, turn off Tool Lock on the Graphics menu.
4. Choose the Text tool.

Figure 15.1: A chart annotated with the drawing tools

5. Refer to Figure 15.1 for the proper location, and drag a text box.

6. Change the text size to 14 points.

7. Type **New Product** and press Enter.

8. Type **Introduction** and click the right mouse button to close the text box.

9. Drag the selection handles of the text block so that the block is not much wider than the text.

10. To center the text inside the text block, choose Text, Justify, and then Center.

11. If necessary, move the text block to the position shown in the figure.

Now, create the ellipse that encloses the text:

12. Choose the Ellipse tool.

13. Click on the Fill tool and select a light gray, solid fill (in the Custom Colors section of the Solid Fill dialog box, choose the second box in the third row).

14. Draw an ellipse around the text. Your text mysteriously disappears...

The Case of the Disappearing Object

On your slide, all objects are layered in the order they were created. Right now, the chart is on the bottom layer, the text is on the middle layer, and the ellipse is on the top. And because the ellipse has a color fill, it is obscuring the text block. The Move to Front and Move to Back tools come to the rescue here; these tools let you change the order of the layers. (*Note:* The Move to Back tool is displayed when you click and hold on the Move to Front tool.)

There are two ways to display the hidden text:

•   Select the ellipse and move it to the back. Note, however, that this action sends the ellipse *all* the way to the back—behind the chart itself. As a result, you won't be able to see the ellipse. You would then need to select the chart and send *it* to the back.

- Select the text and move it the front. This action is more direct, though it does require that you select something that is completely obscured. However, this is not difficult when you know where the hidden object is.

Follow these steps to move the hidden text to the front:

1. Click inside the ellipse. You should see a set of selection handles that represent the text block. If the handles surround the ellipse, you didn't click in the right place. Try again.

2. Click and hold on the Move to Back tool; then drag over to the Move to Front tool. Voila! Your text magically reappears.

Aligning Objects Automatically

Most likely, your text is not exactly centered inside the ellipse. You can manually position the text block, but Harvard gives you a way to align objects automatically: the Align tool. This tool will take two or more objects, and

Align tool

- Center one inside the other—horizontally, vertically, or both

- Align them on the same baseline (bottom, top, left, or right)

To see how this works, use the Align tool to center the text block inside the ellipse in your line chart.

1. Select the text block and the ellipse (hold down Shift as you click on each one).

2. Choose the Align tool, or choose Graphics and then Align.

In the Align dialog box that is displayed, the dotted line in each option indicates where the objects are aligned. Starting with the first option and going clockwise, the alignment points are left, top, centered vertically, bottom, right, and centered horizontally. In our example, we want the objects centered horizontally and vertically. Since you can select only one alignment option at a time, you must take two trips to the Align dialog box.

3. In the Align dialog box, choose the first option in the second row, and click on OK. This option centers the objects horizontally.

4. Select the Align tool again, and choose the second option in the second row. When you click on OK, the text is centered inside the box.

Up Close and Personal

Zoom In tool

For precise positioning of objects, you may want to zoom in on, or magnify, a portion of the screen. The Zoom In and Zoom Out tools let you get "up close and personal" with your graphics. The Zoom In tool magnifies the selected object; or, if no object is selected, it zooms in on the center of the slide. To view a different part of the slide, use the scroll bars. Each time you choose the Zoom In tool, the objects are enlarged to a greater level of magnification. Four levels are available. Figure 15.2 shows your annotation (the text block enclosed in an ellipse) after it has been zoomed in twice.

Zoom Out tool

To reduce the magnification level after you have zoomed in, use the Zoom Out tool. Or, to return the slide to its original size, choose View, Zoom, and then Fit in Window.

Let's zoom in on the annotation, and then draw an arrow from the ellipse to the 1990 data point. This magnification will make it easier to position the arrow in the correct location.

1. With the text block or ellipse selected, choose the Zoom In tool.

2. Choose the Line tool.

3. Click on the bottom edge of the ellipse (see Figure 15.2 for the exact location).

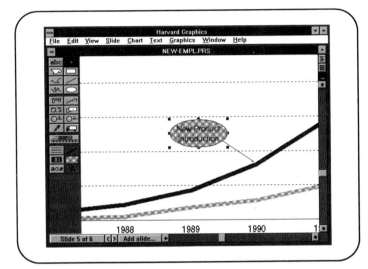

Figure 15.2: The annotation was magnified with the Zoom In tool

4. Move the pointer to the 1990 data point, and click.

5. Choose the Line Attributes tool, and specify a large arrow for Last Ending, and a 1-pt. line thickness. Choose OK.

6. If necessary, adjust the placement and length of the arrow.

7. Preview the slide. It should look like Figure 15.1. The arrowhead may be difficult to see on your screen, but it will print at an acceptable size.

8. Choose the Zoom Out tool to restore the objects to their original sizes.

9. Press Ctrl+S to save the file.

Symbols

Harvard Graphics comes with over 500 clip-art pictures, or *symbols*, that you can use in your presentations. There are pictures of people, animals, buildings, calendars, maps, and other familiar objects, to name just a few. By using symbols in your charts, you don't have to be an artist to add that professional graphics touch.

Related symbols are grouped together in files that have the .SYW file name extension. For example, pictures of animals are stored in ANIMALS.SYW. To see a printout of the symbols, refer to the *Symbols, Palettes, and Presentation Styles* booklet included with your Harvard Graphics documentation.

When you installed Harvard Graphics, you may not have copied all the symbol files. If you need to copy additional symbols, you can use the Install program again (see Step 1). To do the exercises in this chapter, you will need the ANIPLANT.SYW and ARROWS2.SYW symbol files.

Installing symbol files

Using the Symbol Tool

To bring a symbol into a chart, use the Symbol tool in the Slide Editor. When you click on this tool, you are actually loading an external utility program called Symbol Library. This utility prompts you for the name of the symbol file and then displays a window containing each of the symbols stored in this file. Figure 16.1 shows the symbols in the ANIPLANT.SYW file. Once you select a symbol, you can use copy-and-paste commands to bring the symbol into your presentation.

Follow these steps to open a file in Symbol Library:

1. Open your PLAY presentation and add a drawing slide.

2. Choose the Symbol tool. This action loads the Symbol Library program. (You'll notice the window is titled Symbol Library.)

3. In the Open Symbol dialog box, double-click on ANIPLANT.SYW.

4. After a moment, the file is opened in Symbol Library.

5. If necessary, maximize this window. Your screen should look like Figure 16.1.

Viewing a Symbol File

Zooming a symbol

Symbol Library offers three views, available on the View menu: Thumbnail View, List Names, and Zoom Symbol. In Thumbnail view—the default—many different symbols are pictured at once. List Names view displays only the symbol names, and if you click on a name, a picture of the symbol is displayed on the right side of the window. In Zoom Symbol view, the current symbol consumes the entire window; to see the next or previous symbol, press PgDn or PgUp. Another way to zoom a symbol is to double-click on it; double-click the right mouse button to return to Thumbnail view.

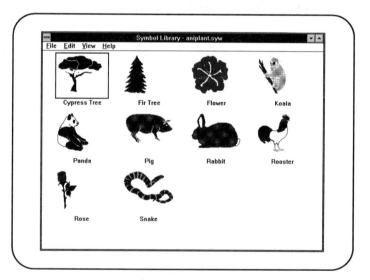

Figure 16.1: The symbols in the ANIPLANT.SYW file

Pasting a Symbol

As mentioned earlier, you bring a symbol into a presentation with the Copy and Paste commands. Just select the symbol (in any view) and choose Copy; then switch to the Harvard Graphics window and choose Paste. Once the symbol is on the slide, you can move and size it.

Let's paste the Rooster symbol into your PLAY presentation.

1. Click on the Rooster symbol.

2. Choose Edit, and then Copy (or press Ctrl+Ins).

3. Minimize the Symbol Library window so that your Harvard Graphics window reappears.

4. Choose Edit and then Paste (or press Shift+Ins). The rooster is dropped onto the middle of the slide.

Pasting Another Symbol

In the preceding exercise, you minimized the Symbol Library window after you copied the symbol. By minimizing the window, as opposed to closing it, you leave the application open and readily available for future use. (If you are copying just one symbol, you can close the Symbol Library window by choosing Exit on the File menu.)

When Symbol Library is still in memory, the Symbol tool works a little differently from the first time you used it. Instead of loading the Symbol Library program and prompting you for a file to open, the tool simply restores the window. The last symbol file you worked with is still displayed, and you can either paste another symbol from this same file or open another file.

Let's open another symbol file in Symbol Library.

1. Choose the Symbol tool. The Symbol Library window reappears, with the ANIPLANT file still displayed.

2. Choose File and then Open.

3. Double-click on ARROWS2.SYW. After a moment, the animal symbols are replaced with arrows.

4. Scroll the window to look at all the different types of arrows.

5. Choose an arrow and copy it to the Clipboard.

6. Minimize the Symbol Library window.

7. Paste the symbol.

8. Drag the symbol to an empty area of the slide.

Resizing a Symbol

Proportional sizing

When you adjust the size of a symbol, you will probably want it to retain its original proportions. To keep a graphic in its original height-to-width ratio as you adjust its size, hold down the Shift key when you drag a selection handle. As you drag, the symbol jumps to the next proportional size. If you don't use the Shift key, the symbol may look distorted (for example, too fat or too thin).

Editing Symbol Elements

Harvard lets you edit and format a symbol's individual elements. For example, you can change the object's outline or fill colors, or delete part of the symbol. The first time you click on the symbol, the entire symbol is selected. Subsequent clicks select individual elements of the symbol.

Creating a Symbol

If you've struggled to create a complicated design (such as a logo), consider making it into a symbol. That way, whenever you want to use this design, you simply paste it from Symbol Library—just as you would any other symbol. Creating and perfecting your design is the hard part. Making a symbol out of it is simply a matter of pasting the design into a new or existing symbol file. Here's how:

1. Select all elements of the design.

2. Press Ctrl+Ins to copy the symbol-to-be.

3. In the Symbol Library window, create or open the target file for the new symbol.

4. Press Shift+Ins to paste. When prompted, enter a name for the symbol. The symbol is pasted at the end of the file.

5. Save the file.

Your symbol is now available to be pasted into any presentation, using the copy-and-paste routine you have already learned.

Closing the Symbol Library Window

Symbol Library remains in memory until you close the window. When you no longer need to add symbols, close the Symbol Library window, with one of the following techniques:

- Click on the minimized application, and choose Close from the menu that pops up.

- With Symbol Library's window displayed, double-click on its Control Menu box.

- Choose File and then Exit from Symbol Library's menu.

Use one of the above methods to close Symbol Library now.

If a picture is worth a thousand words, a color picture might be worth two thousand. Windows 3.0 is responsible for a tremendous surge in color computing, and Harvard Graphics for Windows takes full advantage of it. As you have already seen, Harvard provides the means to change the color of individual components. For example, in Step 3 you chose a different color for the slide title, and in Step 7 you assigned a new color to a pie slice. Here in Step 17 you will see how to globally change the color of an entire presentation, as well as color just the background of the slides.

Using Palettes

If you are a bit fuzzy on what graphics and drawing programs mean by the word *palette*, just consider the original definition: A palette is the big round platter on which painters place and mix dabs of the various paints they use. That palette provides ready access to several colors of paint. Many artists will use several palettes at once, each one containing a different set of colors.

And so it is with Harvard Graphics. The various color palettes included with the program provide a set of colors, each with varying hues and shades. Proper use of Harvard's color palettes will give you the set of colors most effective for your presentation.

Chart Colors vs. Custom Colors

You will recall that the Solid Color dialog box contains two sets of colored squares—Chart Colors and Custom Colors (see Figure 17.1). So far, you have used just the Custom colors, and this is probably the simplest way to assign colors to objects: You select the object, choose the Fill tool, and then select the desired Custom color. You will use this technique whenever you want to change the color of a single element on a single slide. The Custom colors remain largely the same, regardless of which palette is used.

Fill tool

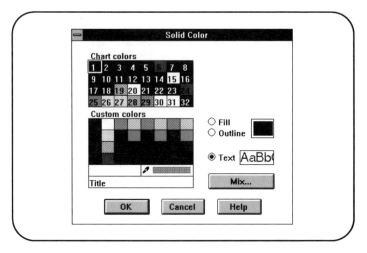

Figure 17.1: To change the color of an object, assign a Custom color from the Solid Color dialog box

Color codes

The Chart colors, on the other hand, are the ones automatically assigned to each slide element. As you can see in Figure 17.1, each Chart color is coded with a number, 1 through 32. These numbers represent particular slide elements. For instance, Harvard designates color box 1 to be for slide titles, color box 2 for the first subtitle, color box 3 for the second subtitle, and so on. To see the element associated with each numbered box, click on the box and read the description at the bottom of the Custom Colors section. Or, refer to the Quick Reference Guide included with Harvard Graphics.

Chart colors are a product of the current palette. By bringing in a new palette, you instantly change the color of all elements in the presentation that use Chart colors. This is how you can globally change the color of all your titles, subtitles, lines, pie slices, vertical bars, and so forth.

Applying a New Palette

To apply a new palette, choose Slide, Color Palette, and then Apply. Palettes are stored in files, and the dialog box shown in Figure 17.2 is simply a gateway to the list of palette files that Harvard installs.

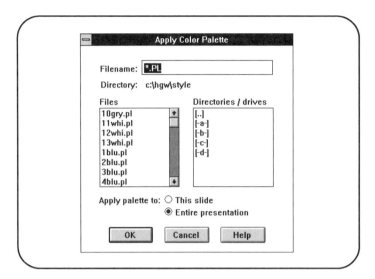

Figure 17.2: Applying a new palette is as simple as recalling a file

By applying one that is different from the default palette (DEFAULT.PL), you change the color definitions of the 32 squares in Chart Colors. Note that objects assigned to a Custom color are *not* affected by a color palette change.

Harvard's palettes are named so that you have some idea of what you're getting. The ones that begin with HR are for high-resolution systems that can show at least 256 colors at once. The abbreviated color name, like CYN for Cyan, indicates what the predominant color theme is for that palette. There are also two monochrome palettes, MONOB and MONOW, that contain only white, black, and shades of gray. Use these palettes when printing to a monochrome printer; that way your screen will closely reflect your printed output.

Palette names

If you didn't copy all the palette files during installation, you can select additional ones by rerunning Install (see Step 1).

On your own, open NEW-EMPL, apply a new palette, and watch how all elements in the presentation instantly change color. To return to the original color scheme, apply DEFAULT.PL.

Editing Colors

While it's likely that the 32 squares in Chart colors will fill your design needs, you may not be satisfied with the particular colors that Harvard provides in each palette. Your favorite 32 colors might include 10 colors from one palette, 15 from another, and 7 from three other palettes. Harvard Graphics gives you total control over the colors in those 32 little squares; you can even mix your own.

The simplest way to edit your Chart colors is to borrow from the Custom colors. The 32 Custom colors represent a broad sampling of colors, and it's likely that you'll find some to your liking there. As you've already seen, you can certainly use a Custom color just the way it is for spot changes, but if you want to apply a Custom color globally to objects already assigned a Chart color, you'll need to take the Custom color and promote it to the Chart section.

Suppose you want to change all of your titles to a different color (red). Here is what you would do:

1. Choose Slide, Color Palette, and then Edit. You'll see the Edit Color Palette dialog box shown in Figure 17.3.

2. Under Apply Chart Colors To, click on the Entire Presentation button.

The color you want is red in the second row of Custom Colors. Also, remember that all titles are assigned Chart color 1, so that is the one you want to change.

3. Click and hold over the red square in Custom Colors, and drag it on top of Chart Colors box 1. The color of that square promptly changes to red.

4. Choose OK.

Now scroll through the presentation, and notice that all titles have taken on the new color assigned to Chart color 1.

Saving palettes

If you want to use this modified color palette in other files, you must save it. Choose Slide, Color Palette, Save, and then enter a file name.

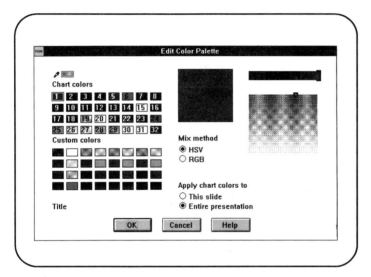

Figure 17.3: Use the Edit Color Palette dialog box to change color assignments

Mixing Colors

If the Chart or Custom colors don't offer the particular color you want to use, you can mix your own in the Edit Color Palette dialog box (Figure 17.3). There are two methods for mixing colors: HSV (Hue/Saturation/Value) and RGB (Red/Green/Blue). For complete instructions on mixing colors, see Chapter 18 in your *Using Harvard Graphics for Windows* documentation.

Coloring the Slide Background

Changing the color of an object is a straightforward task; you select the object and choose the Fill tool. Coloring the slide background is done a bit differently, since you can't select the background. To assign a solid color to the background, choose Slide, Background, Set Fill, and then Solid. You will then see the now-familiar Solid Colors dialog box. At this point, you can choose the desired color.

Another way to change the background color of all slides in the presentation is to edit the color palette as described in the previous section. The background is assigned to color box 30; in the Edit Color Palette dialog box, just drag the desired Custom color to box 30.

Filling the Background with Gradient Colors

A *gradient* is a gradual blending of two hues. To use a gradient fill in the slide background, choose Slide, Background, Set Fill, and then Gradient. Harvard will blend the Start Color you specify with the End Color. By default, the colors are blended from top to bottom. However, you can angle the gradient by using the angle dial in the Gradient Options dialog box.

Here's the scene: You've just finished designing a bar chart—it looks great and you're proud. You chose a font that works well, gave the chart a nice 3-D effect, and kept the various elements clean and well defined. You like the overall design so much that you decide to use it for all of your bar charts. The only problem is that it took you over 10 minutes to produce, and you can't afford to spend that kind of time for each of your charts.

Happily, you don't have to, for Harvard lets you put your designs in a bottle. You can create *templates* (formats) from your own work and then use them over and over again. Once you have the template, you never have to worry about whether your slides are formatted consistently—the template ensures it.

Default Templates

Actually, you have already used templates, perhaps without realizing it. Each time you add a slide, Harvard uses a default template appropriate for the type of chart you are creating. To see what these default templates look like, follow these steps:

1. Open the NEW-EMPL presentation.

2. Choose the Add Slide button.

3. Turn on the Show Slide Template check box.

4. Click on each slide type, and look at the sample box on the right to see a miniature view of the template. From this sample you can get an idea of whether the chart is two- or three-dimensional, where the legend is positioned, if there are grid lines, and so forth.

5. Since you don't want to create a slide at this time, choose Cancel.

In this Step, you will see how you can modify these default templates so they contain the settings you use most often.

Designing a Template

To create a template of your own design, you begin by creating a slide in the usual manner. If you have an existing slide that already has the settings you want to store in the template, you can use this chart.

What kind of things can you store in a template?

- Chart options (legend placement, bar/area style, grid settings, bar width—anything from the Chart Options dialog box)

- Font, size, typestyle, and color for each text area (title, subtitle, labels, and so forth)

- Symbols and other graphic elements added with the drawing tools

- Color palette

- Slide background

Once you format a slide with all the settings you want to store in the template, you create the template with the following command: Slide, Slide Template, and then Create From Slide. You will then be prompted for a template name.

Template Names

There are two types of names you can assign to templates. You can use the following default names, or you can assign your own custom names; each type of name has its own purpose. The 12 default template names are

Default template names

Title	Line
Bullet	Area
Table	High/Low/Close
Pie	Scatter

Vertical Bar	Organization
Horizontal Bar	Drawing

To permanently change the default settings for a certain chart type, give your template one of the names listed just above. As you can see, there is a standard format for each of the 12 slide types. Harvard automatically uses the appropriate template whenever you add a slide. For example, when you add a bullet slide, Harvard uses the options stored in the Bullet template.

On the other hand, when you are creating custom templates for a special project, you'll want to assign unique, descriptive names to your template files; for these, use names other than the ones listed above. You must issue a command whenever you want to use your custom templates—they are not applied automatically. The following section, "Applying Templates," explains how this works.

Custom templates

In these next steps, you will create a template for bullet charts.

1. Go to Slide 2 in NEW-EMPL, the bullet chart.

2. Format the title in Dutch 801.

3. Draw a horizontal line under the title (use the Line tool).

4. Choose Slide, Slide Template, and then Create From Slide.

At this point, you have a decision to make. Do you want to store these bullet chart settings in the Bullet template or under a custom name? If you want every bullet chart in this presentation to have the same bullet and text attributes, use the default name, Bullet. That way, the settings will automatically be used for any new bullet charts you create. If you plan to have several styles of bullet charts in the presentation, however, assign a unique name to the template. For this example, let's use the latter method.

5. In the Slide Template Name field, type **Bullet2**.

6. OK the box.

Applying Templates

As previously mentioned, the default templates are automatically applied to new slides—unless you explicitly specify that you want to use a custom template. How you do this depends on whether you are applying the template to a new or an existing slide.

Applying Custom Templates to New Slides

To apply a custom template to a new slide, don't select a slide type from the Add Slide dialog box. Instead, choose the Custom Template button, and select the name of the template you want to use. After you enter data for the new slide, you will see that the chart conforms to the settings in your custom template. It will automatically have the slide background, color palette, chart options, and graphic elements that you stored in the template. How's that for efficiency?

Applying Templates to Existing Slides

If you want to apply a template to a slide you have already created, display the slide in the Slide Editor and choose Slide, Slide Template, and then Apply. You can then select the template name from the list of slide templates; custom names are always at the bottom of the list. Figure 18.1 shows two bullet charts. The first one uses the default Bullet template. The second one is the same chart after the Bullet 2 template was applied. Notice the difference in bullet shapes and the way the title is formatted.

Keep Existing Chart Options

Before you OK the Apply Slide Template dialog box, note the status of the Keep Existing Chart Options check box. When the box is not marked, Harvard applies all elements that are stored in the template; the template's chart options will override the options in the current chart. When the Keep Existing Chart Options box is marked, the chart's text attributes and formatting options remain intact after applying the template. The only elements that are applied from the template are the slide background, color palette, and graphic objects. When you apply custom templates, most of the time you'll want to turn off Keep Existing Chart Options.

Agenda

- Sales Background
- Corporate Structure
- Work Force Representation
- Benefits

Agenda

◆ Sales Background
◆ Corporate Structure
◆ Work Force Representation
◆ Benefits

Figure 18.1: The top chart uses Harvard's default Bullet template settings; the bottom chart uses a custom template

Step 19

Presentation Styles

15

In Step 18 you saw how Harvard's templates can help you duplicate your slide designs once you have established them, ensuring that you maintain consistency within a slide show. You can control the look of your presentations to an even greater degree with the use of Harvard's *presentation styles*. A presentation's set of templates (default and custom), as well as the default background, color palette, and font, can be saved in a file and used in other presentations.

Creating a Presentation Style

Let's say that NEW-EMPL is to be one of five presentations that Tactile Toys is preparing. To portray an image of a unified organization, you intend to use the same design for each. Harvard's presentation style feature is ideal for this type of cloning. In the following steps, you will create a style and save it under a specific name.

So you can clearly observe the effects of saving and applying styles, you will make three distinct changes to the presentation: You will apply a new color palette, change the background to a gradient fill, and select the font used for all text.

1. Open the NEW-EMPL presentation and promptly save it under a different name, like NEW-PRES.

2. Choose Slide, Color Palette, and then Apply.

3. Choose PLOTTER.PL and click on OK. The new palette changes many elements of your presentation, as you can plainly see with a browse through your slides.

4. Choose Slide, Background, Set Fill, and then Gradient.

5. For Start Color, choose white from Custom Colors; for End Color, choose pale yellow.

6. Choose OK, and notice that your new background has been applied to the entire presentation.

*Default
font*

7. To change the font used in the presentation, choose Slide, Change Presentation Font, and then Dutch 801.

8. Save the presentation.

You have now made several significant changes to the style of your presentation. To use this design in another file, you need to save it as a presentation style. That's easy:

1. Choose Slide, Presentation Style, and then Save. The .STY files listed here are provided by Harvard during installation. We'll discuss them later in "Using the Sample Styles."

2. At Filename, type **TACTILE**.

3. Choose OK.

Applying a Presentation Style

Designing the style is the hard part—applying it is easy. That, of course, is the whole idea: It might take you two weeks to come up with a design that is just right, but once done, duplicating it requires all of 10 seconds, as shown here:

1. Open the NEW-EMPL presentation.

2. Choose Slide, Presentation Style, and then Apply. The Apply Presentation Style dialog box is shown in Figure 19.1.

3. Scroll the list of styles and select TACTILE.STY.

4. Make sure the Keep Existing Chart Options box is marked (more on this in a moment).

5. Choose OK, and then choose OK again to verify that you are changing all slides.

Suddenly, NEW-EMPL looks like NEW-STYLE. Browse through the slides and notice that the background has a gradient fill, all text is Dutch 801, and a different color palette is in effect. All of these changes were the result of applying the TACTILE style.

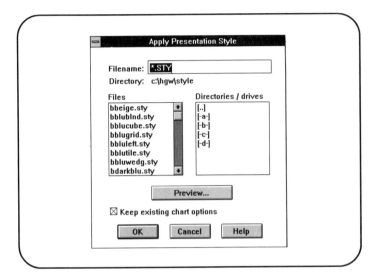

Figure 19.1: In this dialog box you can change the look of an entire presentation

6. Apply TACTILE.STY again, but this time turn off Keep Existing Chart Options.

Because this time you did not keep existing chart options, all charts have taken on the formats of the default templates. If you want to keep your slides' formatting intact when applying a presentation style, make sure Keep Existing Chart Options is marked.

Using the Sample Styles

Depending on the type of Harvard Graphics installation you chose in Step 1, you'll have from 1 to 54 files in your HGW\STYLE directory. The table below describes which files are installed for each type of installation:

All files   Copies all 54 presentation styles

Minimum file set   Copies only the default presentation style (DEFAULT.STY)

Selected files   Copies all, none, or some presentation
                        styles (you choose)

If you didn't copy all the presentation styles, and you wish to do so
now, you can run the Install program again (see Step 1).

Style
names

All style file names begin with a P or B, designating PostScript or
Bitstream. If you own a PostScript laser printer, or use Adobe Type
Manager (ATM), or are preparing print files for a Linotronic imagesetter, use the files that begin with P. The style names that begin with a
B use the fonts that came with Harvard Graphics. Some of the styles have
names that are identical except for the first letter; these styles have the
same settings—except for the types of fonts they use. In other
words, PWHITE1 is the same as BWHITE1, except PWHITE1 uses
PostScript fonts and BWHITE1 uses Bitstream fonts.

The remaining letters in the style names suggest the background
color, pattern, or image. For instance, BPEBBLE.STY has a bitmap
image of pebbles in the background. (Note: You can only see the
pebbles on a high-resolution monitor.)

Changing the Default Presentation Style

When you begin work on a new presentation, Harvard automatically loads the default presentation style (DEFAULT.STY). If you
find that you are frequently changing your slides and overall presentation to a different set of formats, you should create a new
presentation style with these settings and specify it as the default.
That way, whenever you create a new presentation, its default
options and formats will be the ones you most commonly use.

To specify a different name for the default presentation style, choose
Preferences from the File menu. Then, next to Default Presentation
Style, enter the desired file name.

Step 20

Importing/Exporting Data

30

No one lives in a vacuum, not even a dedicated Harvard Graphics user. Sooner or later you will probably need to transfer files back and forth between Harvard and other software programs. For example, the data you want to graph in Harvard may have already been typed in a word processor or spreadsheet program. Rather than retyping it in Harvard, you can import the data. Likewise, you may want to include a Harvard Graphics chart in a word-processed or desktop-published report.

In this step we'll look at the two ways Harvard offers to import and export data.

- Using the Windows Clipboard, you can copy and paste text and graphics between programs.

- With the Import and Export commands on the File menu, you can use disk files to transfer data.

Importing Spreadsheet Data

Why would you want to use Harvard Graphics to create charts of your spreadsheet data if the spreadsheet program itself has built-in graphing capability? First of all, graphs created in a dedicated graphics program are superior to those created in a spreadsheet program. In Harvard you have more options to choose from, and the output quality is much higher. Second, you can use Harvard's ScreenShow feature to present the slides. No spreadsheet program can do that.

Using the Clipboard

If you are using a Windows-based spreadsheet, such as Excel or 1-2-3 for Windows, you can use the Windows Clipboard to copy the data into a Harvard data form. Here's how it works:

1. In your spreadsheet program, create or open the spreadsheet.

2. Select the cells containing the desired data.

3. Choose Edit and then Copy (or press Ctrl+Ins) to copy the data to the Clipboard.

4. Switch to Harvard, and display the data form into which you want to paste the data. (You may need to add a slide.)

5. If the text you are importing contains legends as well as data, make sure that your cursor is at the top-left of the data form, *above cell A1*.

6. To paste the data, choose Edit and then Paste (or press Shift+Ins). Harvard places each spreadsheet cell into a data form cell.

Using the Import Command

The Import command is another way of importing spreadsheet data into Harvard. This command has several advantages over the Clipboard method:

*   It's more versatile. You can import data from DOS- and Windows-based spreadsheets. As long as the file is in 1-2-3 or Excel format, you can import the data.

*   It's potentially faster. Assuming the worksheet already exists as a file, you can import the data with a single operation. With the Clipboard method, you have to launch the application, open the worksheet, copy the data, return to Harvard, and paste the data.

*   You can create a link between the data in the original file and the Harvard chart. Thus, whenever the source file changes, the Harvard chart automatically reflects the new data.

Before you access the Import option, display the data form, and position the cursor in the first cell into which you want to import data.

Figure 20.1 shows the Import dialog box. Your first step to importing is to choose the appropriate file format (Excel or Lotus) from the File Format drop-down list, and then navigate to the appropriate directory. Harvard will display a list of files with .XLS or .WK* extensions. After you click on the desired file, you can choose to Import All Data or do a Selective Import. With Selective Import, Harvard displays a dialog box in which you select a range by row and column coordinates, or by range name.

Importing a range

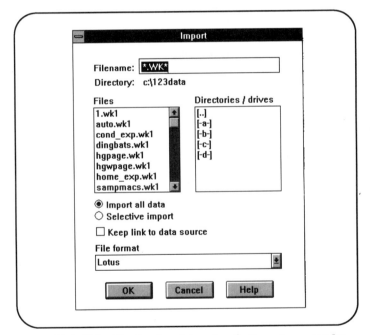

Figure 20.1: If the file already exists, using the Import command to retrieve the spreadsheet data is usually faster and easier than the Clipboard

Note that Harvard can import data from any version of 1-2-3 (1A, 2.x, 3.x, and Windows), but the file name must have a .WKS or .WK1 extension. Thus, if you are using 1-2-3 Release 3.x or 1-2-3 for Windows, you must save the file with the extension .WK1.

Warm Links and Hot Links

As mentioned, you can instruct Harvard to remember the origins of imported data and establish a *link* between the chart and its source file. Harvard uses two types of link: In a *warm link,* Harvard remembers the file from which data is imported, and modifications to that file are reflected in the presentation the next time it is opened. In a *hot link,* when you open a presentation, Harvard automatically loads the program that created the data, and subsequent changes made to the original data are reflected in the presentation immediately.

Creating a Warm Link

Keep Link to Data Source

Harvard can establish a warm link with any program that produces importable chart data—all it needs is a file to latch onto. Creating a warm link couldn't be easier: Just turn on the Keep Link to Data Source check box in the Import dialog box.

Once you do this, whenever you open the presentation, Harvard stops and asks you, "Update Links to Outside Data?" If you answer Yes, Harvard imports the data again from the external file. So if the data has changed, you will get the most current information without having to manually change or reimport the data. If you answer No, Harvard builds the chart from whatever numbers were present the last time you saved.

If you don't always want to chart the most current numbers, you'll appreciate the fact that Harvard asks you about updating each time you open a presentation. But if you know you always want up-to-date numbers, you can tell Harvard to stop asking you. Choose File, then Preferences, and unmark the last option, Prompt to Update Data Links. This tells Harvard to always check links to external files and provide current data, without requiring confirmation.

If you have critical information being supplied to a Harvard chart, warm links are nothing short of miraculous. You can be confident that when you recalculate a spreadsheet, your presentation will get the current numbers, too.

Creating a Hot Link

What makes a link hot as opposed to warm? Warm links establish "loose" connections between programs; hot links establish immediate connections. When you create a hot link, Harvard sees data changes as soon as they occur, not just when the presentation file is next opened. To accomplish this, the program responsible for the data is placed in memory along with Harvard.

Harvard cannot hot-link with just any program—the other program must support *Dynamic Data Exchange* (DDE), the official term for hot-linking. Programs that support hot links include Ami Professional, Excel, 1-2-3 for Windows, and Word for Windows. To establish a hot link, you use the Clipboard's copy-and-paste routine, with a twist—instead of choosing Paste from Harvard's Edit menu, choose Paste Link. (Choosing Paste transfers just the data. Paste Link creates the hot link.)

Dynamic Data Exchange

By resizing the two linked application windows, you can see portions of both programs, as in Figure 20.2. This isn't required, but it does lets you instantly see the change in your Harvard chart when you change values in the source application (in Figure 20.2, Excel).

Each time you open a linked presentation, you are asked if you want to update links (provided you haven't turned this option off in the Preferences dialog box). If you answer Yes, you are reminded that establishing a hot link requires the starting of another application. Answer Yes again, and Harvard automatically launches the external application and opens the linked spreadsheet.

We suspect that you'll use warm links more often than hot links, however impressive the DDE capability is. Unless you truly need instant updates of data, you might not want to tolerate the annoyance, not to mention the memory drain, of Harvard launching the

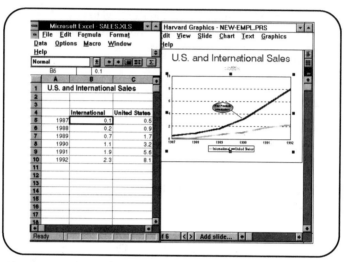

Figure 20.2: The source (Excel) and target (Harvard) applications in resized windows

associated program to establish the hot link. Warm links are less intrusive, because Harvard needs only to check the data in the associated file when the presentation is opened.

Exporting Harvard Graphics Charts

If you want to include a Harvard chart in a word-processed or desktop-published report, you can use the Clipboard (if the other application is Windows-based) or you can use the Export command to convert the chart into a standard format the other program understands. Harvard can export to the following formats:

- Windows Bitmap (.BMP)
- PC Paintbrush (.PCX/.PCC)
- TIFF (.TIF)
- Windows Metafile (.WMF)
- Computer Graphics Metafile (.CGM)
- Micrografx Drawing (.DRW)

Harvard can also create Encapsulated PostScript (EPS) files, but not with the Export command—to do this you must print to a file using a PostScript driver.

To export a slide to another format, you'll need to do the following:

1. In Slide Editor view, display the slide you want to export.
2. From the File menu, choose Export.
3. From the File Format drop-down list, select the type of file to which you want to export.
4. In the Filename field, enter a name for the exported picture.
5. Choose OK.

This converted Harvard Graphics slide can now be imported into PageMaker, Ventura Publisher, WordPerfect, or another program that accepts the file format you chose.

Harvard's export filters are not as accurate as its Clipboard service. Slides exported from Harvard to various formats can produce results that range from acceptable to hilarious. In the WMF and CGM formats, we found many inconsistencies, some minor, some major. PageMaker imported and printed CGM files correctly about half the time, and consistently misplaced text baselines with WMF files. Ventura often refused to print the files at all.

Harvard's difficulty with exporting WMF and CGM files isn't such a problem if your complement of software is Windows based, because you can always use the Clipboard to transfer charts from Harvard to any other Windows application. Moving charts all the way out of Windows, however, requires a clean export to a file, and that's where the problems occur.

Frankly, there is only one avenue available to users of non-Windows programs who want to import Harvard slides as vector-based art: Be rescued by a third party, such as CorelDRAW. If your drawing program has good export filters, then use the Clipboard to import a slide into it. Once there, export it to a file and cross your fingers. Both CorelDRAW and Designer were successful in creating files for WordPerfect and GEM Ventura.

Index

A

Adobe Type manager, 124
aligning
  objects, 99–100
  organization charts, 66–67
  table charts, 30–32
  text, 20
Alt key, 8
angles for pie charts, 48
annotations, 92–93, 97–101
area charts, 54–55, 62, 116
arrows, drawing, 94
attributes
  for bullet charts, 25–27
  for text, 15–20
Autographix Slide Service
    utility, 2
automatic ScreenShows, 84–85
axes, x and y, 51–52, 57, 59

B

backgrounds, 118
  color for, 113–114
  pasting, 74
  for printing, 37
bar charts, 54, 61–62, 117
bitmap fills, 45
Bitstream files, 124
bold text, 17
boxes for organization charts,
    67–68

bullet charts, 23, 116
  attributes for, 25–27
  data for, 24–25
  text for, 27–28
bullet shapes, 25–27
buttons for HyperShows, 85–86

C

cells for table charts, 29–31
characters, formatting, 17–18
Chart Colors, 109–112
Chart Gallery, 23–24, 42
Chart Options command, 46
chart styles, 23
circles, 94
Clear command, 20–21
clip-art, 3, 89, 103–107
Clipboard, 125–126
closing files, 14
clustered bar charts, 61
collapsing outlines, 77–78
color
  for backgrounds, 113–114
  for boxes, 67
  for bullets, 26–27
  editing, 112–113
  for lines, 33, 92
  for objects, 91–92
  palettes for, 109–114, 118
  for pie charts, 43, 45, 48
  for special effects, 20
  for symbols, 106

text boxes, 17
Text tool, 90, 92–93
thickness of lines, 33, 61, 92
3D pie charts, 42
time on axes, 52
title charts, 10–11, 116
Tool Lock option, 91
toolbox, 12
transferring files, 125–131
transition effects, 82–85
tutorial files, 3
typefaces. *See* fonts

U

user interface, 7–14

V

view icons, 12
views
  Outliner, 8–9, 75–80

Slide Editor, 7, 11–13
Slide Sorter, 8, 69–74

W

warm links, 128–129
width
  of bars, 62
  of columns, 32, 43–44

X

XY charts
  data for, 52–54
  options for, 57–62
  parts of, 51–52
  types of, 54–56

Z

zooming, 70–72, 100–101, 104

Selections from The SYBEX Library

DESKTOP PRESENTATION

Harvard Graphics Instant Reference
Gerald E. Jones
154pp. Ref. 726-6
This handy reference is a quick, non-technical answer manual to questions about Harvard's onscreen menus and help displays. Provides specific information on each of the program's major features, including Draw Partner. A must for business professionals and graphic artists who create charts and graphs for presentation.

Harvard Graphics 3 Instant Reference (Second Edition)
Gerald E. Jones
200pp; ref. 871-8
This handy, compact volume is the single complete source for quick answers on all of Harvard's menu options and features. It's small enough to keep on hand while you work—and fast enough to let you keep working while you look up concise explanations and exact instructions for using Harvard commands.

Mastering Animator
Mitch Gould
300pp. Ref.688-X
A hands-on guide to creating dynamic multimedia presentations. From simple animation to Hollywood-style special effects, from planning a presentation to bringing it all to life—it's all you need to know, in straightforward, easy-to-follow terms.

Mastering Harvard Graphics (Second Edition)
Glenn H. Larsen
375pp, Ref. 673-1
"The clearest course to begin mastering Harvard Graphics," according to *Computer Currents*. Readers master essential principles of effective graphic communication, as they follow step-by-step instructions to create dozens of charts and graphs; automate and customize the charting process; create slide shows, and more.

Mastering Harvard Graphics 3
Glenn Larsen
with Kristopher Larsen
525pp; Ref. 870-X
This highly praised hands-on guide uses engaging tutorials and colorful examples to show exactly how to create effective charts, graphs, presentations, and slide shows. Readers create virtually every kind of chart, including many not covered in Harvard's manual. Companion diskette features over $40 worth of clipart—absolutely free.

Teach Yourself Harvard Graphics 3
Jeff Woodward
450pp; Ref. 801-7
A graphical introduction to the hottest-selling presentation graphics program! This illustrated guide leads newcomers through the exact steps needed to create all kinds of effective charts and graphs. There are no surprises: what you see in the book is what you will see on your screen.

Up & Running with Harvard Graphics
Rebecca Bridges Altman
148pp. Ref. 736-3
Desktop presentation in 20 steps—the perfect way to evaluate Harvard Graphics for purchase, or to get a fast, hands-on overview of the software's capabilities. The book's 20 concise lessons are time-coded (each takes no more than an hour to complete), and cover everything from installation and startup, to creating specific types of charts, graphs, and slide shows.

Up & Running with Harvard Graphics 3
Rebecca Bridges Altman
140pp; Ref. 884-X
Come up to speed with Harvard Graphics 3—fast. If you're a computer-literate user who needs to start producing professional-looking presentation graphics now, this book is for you. In only 20 lessons (each taking just 15 minutes to an hour), you can cover all the essentials of this perennially popular progam.

DESKTOP PUBLISHING

The ABC's of the New Print Shop
Vivian Dubrovin
340pp. Ref. 640-4
This beginner's guide stresses fun, practicality and original ideas. Hands-on tutorials show how to create greeting cards, invitations, signs, flyers, letterheads, banners, and calendars.

The ABC's of Ventura
Robert Cowart
Steve Cummings
390pp. Ref. 537-9
Created especially for new desktop publishers, this is an easy introduction to a complex program. Cowart provides details on using the mouse, the Ventura side bar, and page layout, with careful explanations of publishing terminology. The new Ventura menus are all carefully explained. For Version 2.

Desktop Publishing with WordPerfect 5.1
Rita Belserene
418pp. Ref. 481-X
A practical guide to using the desktop publishing capabilities of versions 5.0 and 5.1. Topics include graphic design concepts, hardware necessities, installing and using fonts, columns, lines, and boxes, illustrations, multi-page layouts, Style Sheets, and integrating with other software.

Mastering CorelDRAW 2
Steve Rimmer
500pp. Ref. 814-9
This comprehensive tutorial and design guide features complete instruction in creating spectacular graphic effects with CorelDRAW 2. The book also offers a primer on commercial image and page design, including how to use printers and print-house facilities for optimum results.

Mastering Micrografx Designer
Peter Kent
400pp. Ref. 694-4
A complete guide to using this sophisticated illustration package. Readers begin by importing and modifying clip art, and progress to creating original drawings, working with text, printing and plotting, creating slide shows, producing color separations, and exporting art.

Mastering PageMaker 4 on the IBM PC
Rebecca Bridges Altman, with Rick Altman
509pp. Ref. 773-8
A step-by-step guide to the essentials of desktop publishing and graphic design. Tutorials and hands-on examples explore every aspect of working with text, graphics, styles, templates, and more, to design and produce a wide range of publications. Includes a publication "cookbook" and notes on using Windows 3.0.

Mastering Ventura for Windows (For Version 3.0)
Rick Altman
600pp, Ref. 758-4
This engaging, hands-on treatment is for the desktop publisher learning and using the Windows edition of Ventura. It covers everything from working with the Windows interface, to designing and printing sophisticated publications using Ventura's most advanced features. Understand and work with frames, graphics, fonts, tables and columns, and much more.

Mastering Ventura 3.0 Gem Edition
Matthew Holtz
650pp, Ref. 703-7
The complete hands-on guide to desktop publishing with Xerox Ventura Publisher—now in an up-to-date new edition featuring Ventura version 3.0, with the GEM windowing environment. Tutorials cover every aspect of the software, with examples ranging from correspondence and press releases, to newsletters, technical documents, and more.

Understanding Desktop Publishing
Robert W. Harris
300pp. Ref. 789-4
At last, a practical design handbook, written especially for PC users who are not design professionals, but who do have desktop publishing duties. How can publications be made attractive, understandable, persuasive, and memorable? Topics include type, graphics, and page design; technical and physiological aspects of creating and conveying a message.

Understanding PFS: First Publisher
Gerry Litton
463pp. Ref. 712-6
This new edition of the popular guide to

First Publisher covers software features in a practical introduction to desktop publishing. Topics include text-handling, working with graphics, effective page design, and optimizing print quality. With examples of flyers, brochures, newsletters, and more.

Understanding PostScript Programming (Second Edition)
David A. Holzgang
472pp. Ref. 566-2

In-depth treatment of PostScript for programmers and advanced users working on custom desktop publishing tasks. Hands-on development of programs for font creation, integrating graphics, printer implementations and more.

Up & Running with CorelDRAW 2
Len Gilbert
140pp; Ref. 887-4

Learn CorelDRAW 2 in record time. This 20-step tutorial is perfect for computer-literate users who are new to CorelDRAW or upgrading from an earlier version. Each concise step takes no more than 15 minutes to an hour to complete, and provides needed skills without unnecessary detail.

Up & Running with PageMaker 4 on the PC
Marvin Bryan
140pp. Ref. 781-9

An overview of PageMaker 4.0 in just 20 steps. Perfect for evaluating the software before purchase—or for newcomers who are impatient to get to work. Topics include installation, adding typefaces, text and drawing tools, graphics, reusing layouts, using layers, working in color, printing, and more.

Your HP LaserJet Handbook
Alan R. Neibauer
564pp. Ref. 618-9

Get the most from your printer with this step-by-step instruction book for using LaserJet text and graphics features such as cartridge and soft fonts, type selection, memory and processor enhancements, PCL programming, and PostScript solutions. This hands-on guide provides specific instructions for working with a variety of software.

WORD PROCESSING

The ABC's of Microsoft Word (Third Edition)
Alan R. Neibauer
461pp. Ref. 604-9

This is for the novice WORD user who wants to begin producing documents in the shortest time possible. Each chapter has short, easy-to-follow lessons for both keyboard and mouse, including all the basic editing, formatting and printing functions. Version 5.0.

The ABC's of Microsoft Word for Windows
Alan R. Neibauer
334pp. Ref. 784-6

Designed for beginning Word for Windows users, as well as for experienced Word users who are changing from DOS to the Windows version. Covers everything from typing, saving, and printing your first document, to creating tables, equations, and graphics.

The ABC's of WordPerfect 5
Alan R. Neibauer
283pp. Ref. 504-2

This introduction explains the basics of desktop publishing with WordPerfect 5: editing, layout, formatting, printing, sorting, merging, and more. Readers are shown how to use WordPerfect 5's new features to produce great-looking reports.

The ABC's of WordPerfect 5.1 for Windows
Alan R. Neibauer
350pp; Ref. 803-3

This highly praised beginner's tutorial is now in a special new edition for WordPerfect 5.1 for Windows—featuring WYSIWYG graphics, font preview, the button bar, and more. It covers all the essentials of word processing, from basic editing to simple desktop publishing, in short, easy-to-follow lessons. Suitable for first-time computer users.

The ABC's of WordPerfect 5.1
Alan R. Neibauer
352pp. Ref. 672-3

Neibauer's delightful writing style makes this clear tutorial an especially effective learning tool. Learn all about 5.1's new drop-down menus and mouse capabilities that reduce the tedious memorization of function keys.

The Complete Guide to MultiMate
Carol Holcomb Dreger
208pp. Ref. 229-9
This step-by-step tutorial is also an excellent reference guide to MultiMate features and uses. Topics include search/replace, library and merge functions, repagination, document defaults and more.

Encyclopedia WordPerfect 5.1
Greg Harvey
Kay Yarborough Nelson
1100pp. Ref. 676-6
This comprehensive, up-to-date WordPerfect reference is a must for beginning and experienced users alike. With complete, easy-to-find information on every WordPerfect feature and command—and it's organized by practical functions, with business users in mind.

Mastering Microsoft Word on the IBM PC (Fourth Edition)
Matthew Holtz
680pp. Ref. 597-2
This comprehensive, step-by-step guide details all the new desktop publishing developments in this versatile word processor, including details on editing, formatting, printing, and laser printing. Holtz uses sample business documents to demonstrate the use of different fonts, graphics, and complex documents. Includes Fast Track speed notes. For Versions 4 and 5.

Mastering Microsoft Word 5.5 (Fifth Edition)
Matthew Holtz
650pp; Ref. 836-X
This up-to-date edition is a comprehensive guide to productivity with Word 5.5—from basic tutorials for beginners to hands-on treatment of Word's extensive desktop publishing capabilities. Special topics include style sheets, form letters and labels, spreadsheets and tables, graphics, and macros.

Mastering Microsoft Word for Windows
Michael J. Young
540pp. Ref. 619-7
A practical introduction to Word for Windows, with a quick-start tutorial for newcomers. Subsequent chapters explore editing, formatting, and printing, and cover such advanced topics as page design, Style Sheets, the Outliner, Glossaries, automatic indexing, using graphics, and desktop publishing.

Mastering Microsoft Word for Windows (Second Edition)
Michael J. Young
550pp; Ref. 1012-6
Here is an up-to-date new edition of our complete guide to Word for Windows, featuring the latest software release. It offers a tutorial for newcomers, and hands-on coverage of intermediate to advanced topics, with an emphasis on desktop publishing skills. Special topics include tables and columns, fonts, graphics, Styles and Templates, macros, and multiple windows.

Mastering Microsoft Works on the IBM PC
Rebecca Bridges Altman
536pp. Ref. 690-1
Written especially for small business and home office users. Practical tutorials cover every aspect of word processing, spreadsheets, business graphics, database management and reporting, and basic telecommunications under Microsoft Works.

Mastering MultiMate 4.0
Paula B. Hottin
404pp. Ref. 697-9
Get thorough coverage from a practical perspective. Tutorials and real-life examples cover everything from first startup to basic editing, formatting, and printing; advanced editing and document management; enhanced page design, graphics, laser printing; merge-printing; and macros.

Mastering WordPerfect 5
Susan Baake Kelly
709pp. Ref. 500-X
The revised and expanded version of this definitive guide is now on WordPerfect 5 and covers wordprocessing and basic desktop publishing. As more than 200,000 readers of the original edition can attest, no tutorial approaches it for clarity and depth of treatment. Sorting, line drawing, and laser printing included.

Mastering WordPerfect 5.1
Alan Simpson
1050pp. Ref. 670-7
The ultimate guide for the WordPerfect user. Alan Simpson, the "master communicator," puts you in charge of the latest features of 5.1: new dropdown menus and mouse capabilities, along with the desktop publishing, macro programming, and file conversion functions that have made WordPerfect the most popular word processing program on the market.

Mastering WordPerfect 5.1 for Windows
Alan Simpson
1100pp. Ref. 806-8

The complete guide to learning, using, and making the most of WordPerfect for Windows. Working with a mouse and the Windows graphical user interface, readers explore every software feature, build practical examples, and learn dozens of special techniques—for macros, data management, desktop publishing, and more.

Microsoft Word Instant Reference for the IBM PC
Matthew Holtz
266pp. Ref. 692-8

Turn here for fast, easy access to concise information on every command and feature of Microsoft Word version 5.0—for editing, formatting, merging, style sheets, macros, and more. With exact keystroke sequences, discussion of command options, and commonly-performed tasks.

Microsoft Word for the Macintosh Instant Reference
Louis Columbus
200pp; Ref. 859-9

Turn here for fast, easy access to precise information on every command and feature of Word version 4.0 for the Mac. Alphabetized entries provide exact mouse or key sequences, discussion of command options, and step-by-step instructions for commonly performed tasks.

Teach Yourself WordPerfect 5.1
Jeff Woodward
444pp. Ref. 684-7

Key-by-key instructions, matched with screen-by-screen illustrations, make it possible to get right to work with Word-Perfect 5.1. Learn WordPerfect as quickly as you like, from basic editing to merge-printing, desktop publishing, using graphics, and macros.

WordPerfect 5.1 On-Line Advisor Version 1.1
SYBAR, Software Division of SYBEX, Inc.
Ref. 934-X

Now there's no more need to thumb through lengthy manuals. The On-Line Advisor brings you answers to your Word-Perfect questions on-screen, right where you need them. For easy reference, this comprehensive on-line help system divides up each topic by key sequence,

syntax, usage and examples. Covers versions 5.0 and 5.1. Software package comes with 3½" and 5¼" disks. **System Requirements:** IBM compatible with DOS 2.0 or higher, runs with Windows 3.0, uses 90K of RAM.

Understanding Professional Write
Gerry Litton
400pp. Ref. 656-1

A complete guide to Professional Write that takes you from creating your first simple document, into a detailed description of all major aspects of the software. Special features place an emphasis on the use of different typestyles to create attractive documents as well as potential problems and suggestions on how to get around them.

Understanding WordStar 2000
David Kolodney
Thomas Blackadar
275pp. Ref. 554-9

This engaging, fast-paced series of tutorials covers everything from moving the cursor to print enhancements, format files, key glossaries, windows and MailMerge. With practical examples, and notes for former WordStar users.

Up & Running with Grammatik 2.0
David J. Clark
133pp. Ref. 818-1

Learn to use this sleek new grammar- and style-checking program in just 20 steps. In short order, you'll be navigating the user interface, able to check and edit your documents, customizing the program to suit your preferences, and rating the readability of your work.

Up & Running with WordPerfect Office/Library PC
Jeff Woodward
142pp. Ref. 717-7

A concise tutorial and software overview in 20 "steps" (lessons of 15 to 60 minutes each). Perfect for evaluating the software, or getting a basic grasp of its features. Learn to use the Office PC shell; use the calculator, calendar, file manager, and notebooks; create macros; and more.

Up & Running with WordPerfect 5.1
Rita Belserene
164pp. Ref. 828-9

Get a fast-paced overview of telecommunications with PROCOMM PLUS, in just 20 steps. Each step takes only 15 minutes to an hour to complete, covering the essentials of creating, editing, saving and printing documents; formatting text; creating multiple-page documents; working with fonts; importing graphic images, and more.

Up & Running with WordPerfect 5.1 for Windows
Rita Belserene
140pp; Ref. 827-0

In only 20 lessons, you can start making productive use of the new WordPerfect 5.1 for Windows. Each lesson is pre-timed to take just 15 minutes to an hour to complete. As you work through the book, you'll pick up all the skills you need to create, edit, and print your first document—plus some intermediate and advanced skills for a more professional look.

Up & Running with Word for Windows
Bob Campbell
148pp. Ref. 829-7

This fast-paced introduction will have readers using Word for Windows in no time. The book's 20 lessons or "steps" first cover installation and program navigation, then move on to the essentials of text entry, editing, formatting, and printing. Styles, templates, glossaries, macros, outlines, pictures, and merge letters are also covered.

Up & Running with WordPerfect for Windows
Rita Belserene
140pp. Ref. 827-0

Get a fast-paced overview of telecommunications with PROCOMM PLUS, in just 20 steps. Each step takes only 15 minutes to an hour to complete, covering the essentials of creating, editing, saving and printing documents; formatting text; creating multiple-page documents; working with fonts; importing graphic images; more.

WordPerfect 5 Instant Reference
SYBEX Prompter Series
Greg Harvey
Kay Yarborough Nelson
316pp. Ref. 535-2

This pocket-sized reference has all the program commands for the powerful WordPerfect 5 organized alphabetically for quick access. Each command entry has the exact key sequence, any reveal codes, a list of available options, and option-by-option discussions.

The WordPerfect 5.1 Cookbook
Alan Simpson
457pp. Ref. 680-4

A timesaving goldmine for word processing professionals, this cookbook offers a comprehensive library of sample documents, with exact keystrokes for creating them, and ready-to-use templates on an accompanying disk. Makes full use of version 5.1 features, including PostScript and Laser Jet III support, and covers everything from simple memos to multi-column layouts with graphics.

WordPerfect 5.1 Instant Reference
Greg Harvey
Kay Yarborough Nelson
252pp. Ref. 674-X

Instant access to all features and commands of WordPerfect 5.0 and 5.1, highlighting the newest software features. Complete, alphabetical entries provide exact key sequences, codes and options, and step-by-step instructions for many important tasks.

WordPerfect for Windows 5.1 Instant Reference
Alan Simpson
200pp; Ref. 821-1

This complete pocket reference, tailored specifically for the Windows version of WordPerfect 5.1, provides quick answers to common questions, and step-by-step instructions for using every software feature.

WordPerfect 5.1 Macro Handbook
Kay Yarborough Nelson
532pp, Ref. 687-1

Help yourself to over 150 ready-made macros for WordPerfect versions 5.0 and 5.1. This complete tutorial guide to creating and using work-saving macros is a must for every serious WordPerfect user. Hands-on lessons show you exactly how to record and use your first simple macros—then build to sophisticated skills.

WordPerfect 5.1 Tips and Tricks (Fourth Edition)
Alan R. Neibauer
675pp. Ref. 681-2

This new edition is a real timesaver. For on-the-job guidance and creative new uses, this title covers all versions of WordPerfect up to and including 5.1—streamlining documents, automating with macros, new print enhancements, and more.

OPERATING SYSTEMS

The ABC's of DOS 4
Alan R. Miller
275pp. Ref. 583-2
This step-by-step introduction to using DOS 4 is written especially for beginners. Filled with simple examples, *The ABC's of DOS 4* covers the basics of hardware, software, disks, the system editor EDLIN, DOS commands, and more.

The ABC's of DOS 5
Alan Miller
267pp. Ref. 770-3
This straightforward guide will haven even first-time computer users working comfortably with DOS 5 in no time. Step-by-step lessons lead users from switching on the PC, through exploring the DOS Shell, working with directories and files, using essential commands, customizing the system, and trouble shooting. Includes a tear-out quick reference card and function key template.

ABC's of MS-DOS (Second Edition)
Alan R. Miller
233pp. Ref. 493-3
This handy guide to MS-DOS is all many PC users need to manage their computer files, organize floppy and hard disks, use EDLIN, and keep their computers organized. Additional information is given about utilities like Sidekick, and there is a DOS command and program summary. The second edition is fully updated for Version 3.3.

The ABC's of SCO UNIX
Tom Cuthbertson
263pp. Re. 715-0
A guide especially for beginners who want to get to work fast. Includes hands-on tutorials on logging in and out; creating and editing files; using electronic mail; organizing files into directories; printing; text formatting; and more.

The ABC's of Windows 3.0
Kris Jamsa
327pp. Ref. 760-6
A user-friendly introduction to the essentials of Windows 3.0. Presented in 64 short lessons. Beginners start with lesson one, while more advanced readers can skip ahead. Learn to use File Manager, the accessory programs, customization features, Program Manager, and more.

DESQview Instant Reference
Paul J. Perry
175pp. Ref. 809-2
This complete quick-reference command guide covers version 2.3 and DESQview 386, as well as QEMM (for managing expanded memory) and Manifest Memory Analyzer. Concise, alphabetized entries provide exact syntax, options, usage, and brief examples for every command. A handy source for on-the-job reminders and tips.

DOS 3.3 On-Line Advisor Version 1.1
SYBAR, Software Division of SYBEX, Inc.
Ref. 933-1
The answer to all your DOS problems. The DOS On-Line Advisor is an on-screen reference that explains over 200 DOS error messages. 2300 other citations cover all you ever needed to know about DOS. The DOS On-Line Advisor pops up on top of your working program to give you quick, easy help when you need it, and disappears when you don't. Covers thru version 3.3. Software package comes with 3½" and 5¼" disks. **System Requirements:** IBM compatible with DOS 2.0 or higher, runs with Windows 3.0, uses 90K of RAM.

DOS Instant Reference
SYBEX Prompter Series
Greg Harvey
Kay Yarborough Nelson
220pp. Ref. 477-1
A complete fingertip reference for fast, easy on-line help:command summaries, syntax, usage and error messages. Organized by function—system commands, file commands, disk management, directories, batch files, I/O, networking, programming, and more. Through Version 3.3.

DOS 5: A to Z
Gary Masters
900pp; Ref. 805-X
A personal guru for every DOS 5 user! This comprehensive, "all you need to know" guide to DOS 5 provides detailed, A-to-Z coverage of DOS 5 commands, options, error messages, and dialog boxes—with syntax, usage, and plenty of examples and tips. It also includes hundreds of informative, in-depth articles on DOS 5 terminology and concepts.

SPEED KEYS

File Management

Create new presentation	Ctrl+N
Open presentation	Ctrl+O
Print presentation	Ctrl+P
Save presentation	Ctrl+S

Viewing Slides

Preview slide	F2
View ScreenShow (from beginning)	Ctrl+F2
View ScreenShow (from current slide)	Alt+F2

Formatting

Bold	Ctrl+B
Center object horizontally on slide	Ctrl+H
Chart Options	F8
Italic	Ctrl+I